# B Journey Through the BIBLE

Dr. **Susan Willhauck** works with the Children's Sabbath project of the Children's Defense Fund in Washington, D.C. She is a diaconal minister in the North Georgia Annual Conference of The United Methodist Church, previously serving on staff at McKendree United Methodist Church in Lawrenceville, Georgia. She holds a Doctor of Philosophy in religious education from The Catholic University of America, a Master of Theological Studies in education and ecumenics from Wesley Theological Seminary, and a Bachelor of Arts from Emory and Henry College.

JOURNEY THROUGH THE BIBLE: JOHN. An official resource for The United Methodist Church prepared by the General Board of Discipleship through the division of Church School Publications and published by Cokesbury, a division of The United Methodist Publishing House; 201 Eighth Avenue, South; P.O. Box 801; Nashville, TN 37202. Printed in the United States of America. Copyright ©1995 by Cokesbury. All rights reserved.

For permission to reproduce any material in this publication, call 615-749-6421, or write to Cokesbury, Syndication—Permissions Office, P.O. Box 801, Nashville, TN 37202.

To order copies of this publication, call toll free 800-672-1789. Call Monday–Friday 7:30–5:00 Central Time or 8:30–4:30 Pacific Time. Use your Cokesbury account, American Express, Visa, Discover, or MasterCard.

**EDITORIAL TEAM**
**Debra G. Ball-Kilbourne,**
    Editor
**Linda H. Leach,**
    Assistant Editor
**Linda O. Spicer,**
    Adult Section
    Assistant

**DESIGN TEAM**
**Susan J. Scruggs,**
    Design Supervisor,
    Cover Design
**Teresa B. Travelstead,**
    Layout Designer

**ADMINISTRATIVE STAFF**
**Neil M. Alexander,**
    Vice-President,
    Publishing
**Duane A. Ewers,**
    Editor of Church
    School Publications
**Gary L. Ball-Kilbourne,**
    Executive Editor of
    Adult Publications

 Cokesbury

**Art:** *The Bible in Art: The New Testament* (Hodder and Stoughton, 1904), p. 5; Master of the Catholic Kings, *The Marriage at Cana,* Samuel H. Kress Collection, © 1994 Board of Trustees, National Gallery of Art, Washington, p. 16; Charles Shaw, pp. 48, 63, 72, 80, 89, 97.

# TABLE OF CONTENTS

**Volume 12: John**       **by Susan Willhauck**

11  12  13  14 – 20  19  18

# $\mathcal{J}$NTRODUCTION TO THE SERIES

Welcome to JOURNEY THROUGH THE BIBLE!
You are about to embark on an adventure that can change
your life.

## WHAT TO BRING WITH YOU
Don't worry about packing much for your trip. All you need to bring with
you on this journey are
- an openness to God speaking to you in the words of Scripture
- companions to join you on the way, and
- your Bible

## ITINERARY
In each session of this volume of JOURNEY THROUGH THE BIBLE, first you
will be offered some hints for what to look for as you read the Bible text,
and then you will be guided through four "dimensions" of study. Each is
intended to help you through a well-rounded appreciation and application
of the Bible's words.

## HOW TO PREPARE FOR YOUR JOURNEY THROUGH THE BIBLE
Although you will gain much if all you do is show up for Bible study and par-
ticipate willingly in the session, you can do a few things to gain even more:
- Read in advance the Bible passage mentioned in What to Watch For,
  using the summaries and hints as you read.
- During your Bible reading, answer the questions in Dimension 1.
- Read the rest of the session in this study book.
- Try a daily discipline of reading the Bible passages suggested in
  Dimension 4. Note that the Bible texts listed in Dimension 4 do *not* relate
  to a particular session. But if you continue with this daily discipline, by
  the end of thirteen weeks, you will have read through *all* of that portion
  of the Bible covered by this volume.

Studying the Bible is a lifelong project. JOURNEY THROUGH THE BIBLE
provides you with a guided tour for a few of the steps along your way. May
God be with you on your journey!

Gary L. Ball-Kilbourne
Executive Editor, Adult Publications
Church School Publications

## Questions or comments?
## Call Curric-U-Phone 1-800-251-8591

# John 1:1-18

# The Word Became Flesh

## *What to Watch For*

John 1:1-18 is one of those grand passages of Scripture that sticks in the memory. Known as "the prologue" or overture of the Gospel of John, this passage is a poem or hymn consisting of three stanzas with prose describing the witness of John the Baptist inserted in verses 6-8 and 15. As you read, watch for these emphases:

➤ The author of this Gospel testified to his experience of Christ. He asserted that Jesus was sent by God to redeem humankind.
➤ This text introduces a succession of themes that are developed later in the book. Key words are *Word, light, life, grace,* and *truth.*
➤ John, or "the fourth evangelist" as he is called, made the point that the Word (Jesus Christ), who was with God from the beginning, took the form of a human being. Why? In order that the world might understand who God was and is and will always be. Not everyone accepted Jesus when he came, but those who did received a new, transforming power.

Readers should fasten their seatbelts for a ride through a provocative and challenging Gospel!

## Dimension 1:
## What Does the Bible Say?

1. What does this passage say about "the Word"?

2. What does it say about "the true light"?

3. How would you describe the language in this passage?

4. What do you think is the purpose of this passage? What was the author's intention?

## Dimension 2:
## What Does the Bible Mean?

### A Challenging Passage

This is a familiar Bible passage that remains something of a mystery. While we may have heard it many times, many a student of the Bible has shied away from studying the passage because of its difficulty. Bible scholars interpret this passage in numerous diverse ways. Much has been written about the prologue and the Gospel of John as a whole. (We know that Origen in the third century wrote a commentary on John that exceeded thirty-two volumes, and he wasn't even finished!)

It takes some courage to approach this Gospel, but appproaching it with an open mind may lead one to a new and deeper understanding.

### WHO IS THE AUTHOR?

The church has traditionally held that this Gospel was produced by John, the son of Zebedee, one of the Twelve. It probably was written at Ephesus. Irenaeus (A.D. 177-200, a student of Polycarp, bishop of Smyrna and thought to have been a disciple of John) claimed that this Gospel was indeed written by the apostle John. It is also claimed that John wrote the three letters (1, 2, and 3 John) and Revelation. This view was contested early on in the church by theologians who recognized different styles of writing and varying doctrinal points of view. Some modern Bible scholars propose that the Gospel, as we know it, was the work of more than one editor. There is a lack of solid evidence to draw a final conclusion regarding authorship.

The date of composition is also uncertain. Some declare it to be a product of the late first century (A.D. 90-100) or early second century. Others believe it was earlier. Most agree that it was composed after the Synoptic Gospels (Matthew, Mark, and Luke). At any rate, it may be safe to say that the author had claim to a line of tradition and authority from the earliest of Jesus' followers. This study refers to the author as "John."

## A Gospel of Persuasion

The purpose of the Gospel of John is more certain. Like the Synoptics, the Gospel of John appears to have been written to describe the life and ministry of Jesus Christ. It may have been intended to persuade those in the author's community, who were teetering on the edge, to make a full commitment or to shake up potentially "lukewarm" Christians, giving encouragement to those whose faith was wavering. The author

was a Jew who was part of a community who had broken with the synagogue. He was influenced by Greek culture and perhaps was attempting to write in a way the Greeks could understand.

John's Gospel has been contrasted with Matthew, Mark, and Luke. These are called the "Synoptic Gospels" because they provide a "synopsis" of Jesus' life and ministry. Some have characterized the difference between the Synoptics and John by saying that John is somehow loftier, more theological, or spiritual. Luther called it the "chiefest of the Gospels." John may have been confronted with a different set of issues or problems than the writers of other Gospels. It was his task to interpret, to testify, to witness to his experience of Christ Jesus at a point in time that was crucial for the advancement of the faith.

The language of the prologue—prose and poetry— is forceful. John really wanted to be heard! For him, everything was at stake. At the time John wrote, there were many different religions and philosophies operative in the culture. A prevailing viewpoint maintained that it did not matter what one believed. In contrast, John takes his readers by the collar and shouts, "It does matter!"

## A Gospel of Beginnings

**Gnosticism**

Gnosticism was an early heresy that assumed that the world and all matter was evil. Similarly, the Docetists or "seemists" did not believe that Christ was actual flesh and blood. He only "seemed" human, but could not have been flesh because it was considered evil.

For the moment put parentheses around verses 6-8 and 15. We will come back to those verses later. John, like the Book of Genesis, opens with the words, *En arche*, "in the beginning." If Genesis tells the story of the beginning of the human race, then John tells of new beginnings. John alternates between describing God at the beginning of time and as experienced anew in the birth and life of Jesus Christ. God is portrayed in this Gospel as both *transcendent* (beyond the world) and *immanent* (related to the world).

The text declares that all things were made through God. John expresses the Christian view of the world: If God created it, it must be good. Some ancient religions looked upon the world and flesh as evil and advocated complete disengagement from the world and flesh. John 1:1-18 professes that God created the world and chose to be revealed in flesh. The things of the world are not to be rejected as evil nor are they to be glorified as idols. If we pay attention to John's message, we learn that although there are times when the world seems to be full of evil—when bitterness, hostility, or pain prevail—God loves the creation enough to redeem it.

## The Irony of the Gospel

Verse 1 claims that "the Word was God." Another translation renders this phrase, "what God was, the Word was" (Revised English Bible). "The Word" describes God. The Greek term translated "Word" is *logos*, which not only means "speech," but also means "reason." We get our word *logic*

6

from it. The *logos* has been described as "the mind of God." It was a term familiar in the Greek philosophy of Plato and synthesized into Jewish thought by Philo of Alexandria, a contemporary of Jesus. The author applies the term *Word* as a description of Christ.

This passage is often said to describe the pre-existence of Christ. This is a difficult concept for it does not mean, of course, that Jesus—the man—existed before creation. Rather, "the mind of God" expressed in Jesus tells us what God is like. Jesus was the human form of the mind of God. When we hear in the Gospels of Jesus taking care of "the least of these," he was showing us what God is like. *Logos* represents the self-expression of God. Christ is that self-expression. There was a connection with the Wisdom of God described in the Old Testament. From all eternity God has existed with his Word. One could even say God and Christ are uncreated. Mind-boggling? Yes! We are reminded of a favorite question of children: "If God created us, then who created God?"

In a way, John does not seem reasonable to our critical minds. Therein lies the irony in his Gospel. He wanted to identify God to his listeners, but could only say that there really is no way to pinpoint God. He did not say that God is the eschatological ground of our being. He pointed to the man Jesus, sung a hymn to him, and said, "This is who God is."

God sent Jesus to reveal a message about God. This action has been described many ways. Jesus has been called the great translator, bringing God's word to humankind in a way they could understand, a particularly meaningful explanation in our multicultural, multilingual society. Jesus crosses all human barriers and differences of race, creed, and color. Yet it is also true that the translator in this case is also the message translated. As Bishop William R. Cannon wrote in *The Gospel of John* (Upper Room, 1985), "the messenger is the message."

The Word is described as "life" and "light." In verse 10 John stated that even though the light has come into the world, people do not always accept the light. Similarly, when we hear and accept the Word of God, we are "enlightened." The proverbial light bulb goes off in our heads. It is like getting a new idea that you cannot believe never occurred to you before.

John 1:1-18 describes what is called the incarnation, from *carne* meaning to "become enfleshed." John wrote in verse 14, "And the Word became flesh and dwelt among us" (RSV). Another translation for the word *dwelt* is "pitched his tent" or "tabernacled" with us. These words remind us of God dwelling in the desert with Israel.

## A Strong Christological Statement

John made a strong Christological statement in this passage. (Christology is the part of theology that attempts to explain the identity and nature of Christ. Was he divine or merely human?) John jumped right into the middle of one of the earliest controversies of the church, a controversy that sparked several of the great councils of the church. Perhaps, as some have speculated, John realized that there were some who did not acknowledge Jesus as the revealer of God. John argues otherwise.

In verses 6-8 and 15, the evangelist interjected a statement regarding John the Baptist's role as a witness to the Word. (The text just reads John, but clearly refers to the Baptist.) The writer makes it clear that John the Baptist is not the Word. It may be that the writer knew about and was reacting against a group of people who claimed John the Baptist as the Messiah. Some did not accept Jesus Christ, but those who did gave the power to become offspring of God (verse 12). From Christ we all receive grace (not just a select few). We receive that redeeming love that was a fulfillment of the law of Moses. As "the mind of God," Christ makes God known to us. To all who doubt or question or resist, John spoke: Jesus Christ is for real.

## Dimension 3:
## What Does the Bible Mean to Us?

### A Difficult Notion

Recall your associations with this passage. Are you familiar with it? What memorable sermons have you heard preached on this text? In what way has the prologue spoken to you? In what context have you studied it? What hymns can you find that depict the Incarnation?

"Word made flesh" was a difficult notion to comprehend in John's day, as it is today. In our contemporary situation, what meaning do we derive from this passage? One way to approach the study of this Gospel is to view it as a sermon or a teaching. In light of John's purpose for writing this Gospel, identify yourself and your congregation in the passage. The world of John may seem different from our own, but the message he proclaimed of Jesus Christ stands even today. It is a message that has endured generations. One might even claim that the message has a particular importance in today's world. Can you think of reasons why this might be true? What is that message for today's Christians? What do we learn from this passage? How does it change us?

John's prologue tells us something about the uniqueness and significance of Jesus Christ. Many religions acknowledge incarnations of God. What makes Jesus unique? God is revealed to humanity in various ways, nature and history among them. God is not, however, revealed completely in these ways. John tells us that the decisive revelation of God is Christ. Many of us can think of a favorite spot in God's creation, a beautiful place

8

we like to go to experience the presence of God. It may be the ocean, a mountain chapel, a quiet forest. When we go to these "sacred places," God's presence is never more apparent.

Yet in the desperation of the ghetto, in the "ugly" places, in the streets filled with crime, God may seem absent. God can be experienced in creation, but is most completely known in the person of Jesus. In the love of Christ we see God's presence even in places that are filled with pain. Nobel peace prize winner and nun, Mother Teresa, has cared for the sick and dying for many years in the slums of Calcutta. She has testified often that it is among these people who have been disposed of by society that she most experiences the presence of Christ.

## Life and Light for All

The Word made flesh brought life and light to all. A person can be physically alive and yet dead inside. There is life, and then there is life in Christ. It is common today for persons to reject religion, claiming their life is full without it, that they do not need it. Some prefer to walk in darkness because they have grown used to "going it alone." Even many of Jesus' own people refused to receive the light. Darkness can be terribly attractive in that one does not have to gaze in full light upon one's mistakes. A person's "dark side" can blend in with the darkness. Yet the benefits of light are obvious. We need light and stumble and falter without it.

This incarnational perspective asserts that despite sin, the basic goodness of humanity remains intact. God is revealed in Jesus Christ, but also in us. This reality does not deny the presence of sin and evil within us. The evil can sometimes hide or veil God's presence; when we accept God's presence in our lives, we grow in love and share it with others.

## The Seed of a Doctrine

Even after centuries of theological discussion, we have not exhausted all the nuances of meaning in John's passage. One commentator points out that John's purpose is not so much to prove that Jesus was the Word of God, a true revelation of God, but to share his conviction. It is a conviction that underlies the entire Gospel. The power of John's message, of the Incarnation, is that God is not some far-off, unconcerned deity, but a here-and-now reality. We can honor and praise the pre-existent Word. We can experience the awesome mystery of a transcendent God. We can also know him in a human face, in a human touch. The love we extend to others in the midst of suffering, the daily acts of care and giving—these things embody the love that Christ showed us. As Frederick Bueckner writes in *Wishful Thinking* (Harper and Row, 1973; page 43), one would not expect God to lower himself to our mundane world. It was, in Bueckner's words, a very undignified thing to do. The radicalness of this act cannot be overestimated. Although modern literature has tried to create parables that depict sacrificial love, none can hold a candle to this "greatest story ever told."

The prologue of John is said to be a seed of our doctrine of the Trinity. It places the Word of God as distinguishable but inseparable from God. We confess Jesus to be both human and divine. This does not mean Jesus was "half God, half human." Jesus was a human who experienced human temptation and suffering. His life and ministry, his death and resurrection, prompt us to know and claim him to be the Son of God. His name, Emmanuel, means, "God with us." Our faith in Christ as Son of God is born out of what we know he did, what he taught, what he stood for.

The fourth Gospel demands great faith. Some of us may be prone to feel that the stakes are too high, that John expected too much. Did John expect us to believe just because he said it? After all, it is not easy to understand the ways of God, nor to accept who God is and what he can mean to us personally. We know that Jesus was a historical reality. We know this man lived, and the Gospels record incidents and stories and sayings connected with his ministry. We might even go so far as to affirm with the earliest traditions of the church that Jesus was the revealer of God. We affirm this in our liturgies, creeds, and hymns. Do we affirm it in our hearts? Is it evident in the way we relate to one another in the Christian community? How do we, like John the Baptist, bear witness to the Light in the world?

## Dimension 4:
## A Daily Bible Journey Plan

*Day 1:* **John 1:1-18**

*Day 2:* **John 1:19-28**

*Day 3:* **John 1:29-34**

*Day 4:* **John 1:35-42**

*Day 5:* **John 1:43-51**

*Day 6:* **John 2:1-12**

*Day 7:* **John 2:13-25**

# $\mathcal{E}$NCOUNTERS WITH JESUS

## What to Watch For

In John 2:1-11 we read what appears to be a simple story of a wedding. Almost immediately, however, we get the sense that there is a deeper meaning and significance. John tells this story, which is not told in the other Gospels. As you read this passage, watch for these emphases:

➤ At an ordinary social event, when the wine was about to run out, Jesus miraculously turned the water into wine. This event was called "the first of his signs," which revealed his glory.

➤ During this encounter with Jesus (as in other encounters such as at the cleansing of the Temple), the conversations with Nicodemus and the Samaritan woman attempt to present Jesus as authentic, as one who truly reveals God in his actions.

➤ Like any good storyteller, John tells his readers about his main character a little at a time.

➤ Note that Jesus did not change water into wine in order to "show off." Few present at the wedding even knew about what happened. Also, it was more than a simple act of kindness. Jesus showed us that right in the midst of life, God's transforming power is at work.

1. Describe the conversation between Jesus and his mother concerning the crisis at hand.

2. What did Jesus instruct the servants to do?

3. What was the response of the wine steward to what had happened?

4. What was the purpose of this first sign? Why did Jesus do it? What affect did it have?

## DIVISIONS IN THE GOSPEL OF JOHN

For study purposes, the Gospel of John is often divided into the following sections. It should be noted, however, that the author did not intend such a division:

The Prologue—John 1:1-18

The Book of Signs—John 1:19–12:50

The Book of Glory (including the farewell of Jesus and the death and resurrection of Jesus)—John 13:1–20:31

The Epilogue—John 21:1-25

### It Happened at a Wedding Feast

Cana of Galilee was a village near Nazareth (see the map on the inside back cover). There was a wedding. Mary was there. So were Jesus and some of the disciples. Mary became concerned when the provisions ran low. Perhaps she had something to do with the planning of the event. Early, noncanonized writings (material that the early church did not find authoritative and that were not included in the Scripture) tell more details about the story. One source says that Mary was the sister of the bridegroom's mother. It claims the bridegroom was John and that his mother was Salome, the sister of Mary. The writer of John omits these details.

In ancient Palestine, a wedding feast was a great celebration, and hospitality was taken seriously. Jewish law decreed that the wedding of a virgin was to take place on a Wednesday. The festivities took more than one day. Wine was essential at such a celebration. Grapes, of course, were a main crop of the Middle East. The wine that was drunk may have been a mixture of fermented juice and water. The poor drank very little wine, but a wedding feast was a special occasion. To run out of wine was a disgrace for the wedding families. Mary approached Jesus and told him of the predicament. His reply seemed curt, almost unkind. "Woman," he said, "what concern is that to you and to me? My hour has not yet come" (4). "Woman," or *gunai* in the Greek, was not the harsh, disrespectful term that it seemed. Jesus also used this term in 19:26 when he was dying. The phrase *what to me and you* was a kind of Jewish saying or expression that was used either to mean that something was none of your business or that it was not something to worry about or to be concerned with. Was Mary asking Jesus for a miracle? Was she requesting Jesus to use his power to produce more wine? More than one scholar has suggested that it was not necessarily expected that the Messiah would have miraculous powers. Mary may have simply been reporting the situation. Yet it does seem that she expected some kind of response from Jesus. She was concerned for the needs of those at the party. She looked to Jesus, whom she knew to be unique. To this day, some Christians continue to see Mary as one who intercedes on our behalf.

## More Than a Simple Story

This tale is much more than a simple story about human need being met. It is more than a mere act of compassion. Although Jesus was deeply concerned about human need, in this case Jesus was probably not governed by such concerns. "Woman, what concern is that to you and to me?" he questioned. Clearly, Jesus was governed only by God. No one can bring God unto themselves by their own efforts. No one can control God by special privilege or claim, not even Jesus' mother. God always takes the initiative. Jesus did not act because others expected him to act. "My hour has not yet come," he replied. Mary seemed to understand Jesus' intent in her next statement to the servants, "Do whatever he tells you." Jesus then acted in a way that revealed God, disclosing how God can transform all things.

As God's Son, Jesus was devoted to revealing the truth of God. On many occasions Jesus spoke of "his hour." In many cases the hour refers to the time of his death. The identity and significance of Jesus was not revealed all at once, but in stages. Jesus did not say to the crowd, "Hey, look what I can do. I can turn water into wine. That shows I am the Son of God." The time was not right for that. His hour had not yet come.

In verse 7 Jesus told the servants to fill the water jars with water. The water jars were used for ceremonial cleaning of feet and hands upon entry to the house—a rite dictated by Jewish law. The water that was originally in the jars had been used for this purpose, indicating that the party was in full swing.

The six jars each contained twenty to thirty gallons of water. In verse 8 Jesus instructed the servants to draw some of the liquid from the jars and take it to the chief steward. When the steward tasted it, he discovered that the water had become wine, and he expressed bewilderment. He wondered where this new wine, the good wine, had come from. The wine steward remarked with humor in verse 10 that most people use up the good stuff first and later bring out the cheap stuff when people have drunk enough that their sense of taste is dulled. Instead, at this wedding celebration, it appeared the best was saved for last. Why would Jesus turn 150 to 180 gallons of water into wine? Details need not bother us. The transforming power of Christ and the abundance of his blessing is at issue here.

## Signs of Jesus

One interpretation of this passage is that the water of purification in Jewish law was inadequate. The six jars were an incomplete number. Seven is the number of wholeness and completion in Judaism. Therefore, the water of one age was replaced by the good wine of another. Because water was a valuable commodity in the arid Middle East, rather than throwing out the water, Jesus transformed it. He took something good, basic, and fundamental to life and made it better, richer, tastier. The ceremonial rites of Jewish law were good and basic to Judaism. Jesus made "new wine" to fulfill, to provide for, and to transform persons.

According to John, this first sign of Jesus revealed his glory and his disciples believed in him (verse 11). *Sign* is an important word in John's vocabulary. From the Greek word *semeion* it refers to a symbolic action that points to the purpose of God. A sign is a remarkable deed in which God's presence and power is evident. This sign of changing water into wine was not a "showy" thing meant to prove something to the crowd. It was the first of several signs that pointed the way to John's readers. Like road signs, they lead us somewhere. When Jesus' hour had come, those who knew him looked back at his life. They understood that each aspect of his life pointed to who he was and his message.

14

# SIGNS OF JESUS

While there is debate about which of Jesus' actions can be classified as "signs," those actions traditionally understood in this light include
1. The wedding at Cana
2. The healing of the officer's son at Cana
3. The healing of the paralytic at Bethesda
4. The feeding of the five thousand at Galilee
5. Walking on the water at Galilee
6. The healing of a blind man in Jerusalem
7. The raising of Lazarus at Bethany

## His Hour Had Not Yet Come

The sign "revealed his glory" (11). What is Jesus' glory? Simply put, it is his divine nature that evokes awe and reverence. This was one sign that showed Jesus' glory in its fullness, but there would be more to come, for "his hour had not yet come" (4). Jesus was aware that many people who witnessed his signs were still not satisfied. They were looking for supernatural proof before they could believe. Jesus did not perform signs and wonders for this purpose, and he chided those who kept looking for proof. Persons who need signs and miracles in order to believe usually keep asking for more. The Gospels contain many accounts of those who witnessed his miracles and yet still did not believe. In fact, for some the signs had the opposite effect because upon seeing Jesus doing these things they concluded he was Beelzebub, or the Evil One.

When people saw the miracles occur, some of them already had some faith, and the miracles served to deepen their faith. Others, who did not know Jesus, saw the miracles and found that they served to open the door to Christian conviction. This story is not concerned with **how** the transformation of water to wine took place. To ponder whether or not water was chemically turned into wine and how this was done misses the focus of the story. The primary focus is not on the miracle, but on the glory of Jesus revealed in the sign.

Jesus was on a mission. Why would he trouble himself to perform a miracle at someone's wedding? After all, running out of wine is certainly not a life-and-death matter. Why would Jesus have taken the time to attend a wedding feast? In his action, Jesus was doing more than merely replenishing wedding refreshments. He was showing us what God is like. God will do what is necessary. God will transform. God will provide abundantly for people.

### Weddings . . . Celebrations of Love

Visualize the scene depicted in the fifteenth century painting "The Marriage at Cana." How do you imagine it? A wedding is a joyous occasion. Can you picture Jesus talking and laughing among the guests? Do we fail to view Jesus as a human being who participated in family and social life?

John chose this scene carefully. He included this story for a reason. It was part of the tradition he had received about Jesus, and he deemed it significant. The scene was a wedding, a happy occasion, but not uncommon. Sometimes people today jokingly remark at weddings,

"Well, the party's over now" or "Your life is over." Despite the humor, most persons find weddings a cause for celebration. In the Jewish-Christian traditions weddings have a significance beyond that of two people getting "hitched." They are a public celebration of the couple and the faith community. It is a celebration of the love—the love of the couple and the love of God. A wedding is a good place, a good time for a sign.

Imagine the potential for embarrassment in this scene. Everyone wants their wedding to be perfect. Can you recall a time when you were a host at a social gathering or in charge of some event and something went wrong?

Have you ever panicked when faced with such a mishap? How did you or others respond to remedy the situation?

## Explore the Clues

John's style is not to lay things out in ABC order. John was the consummate storyteller. He said what he wanted to say in a story. The situation and characters drew out various aspects of Jesus to lead John's readers to a response. John wanted his readers to gather up the clues and details from his stories and put them together. What are the clues in this story?

● First, there was the conversation between Jesus and Mary. Was Jesus angry or disrespectful? Was he having so much fun that he did not want to be bothered? Perhaps he was just emphatic. He was not pressured into doing what people think he should have done. His purpose was God's purpose. How often do we put our wants and desires over God's? When we pray, do we ask God to "do this or do that" for us? Is Jesus' purpose just to meet our needs? Are we disappointed and do we lose interest in religion when our wants and desires are not met? How can we better understand Jesus' purpose and what he does for us?

Mary has an important role in the story. She made the situation and need known. Perhaps she initiated the miracle. Who are the people in your own life who fulfill a role of interceding for or initiating miracles? Have you ever been able to act in this capacity?

● Another clue lies in the report of what Jesus eventually did. In spite of his reply, "My hour has not yet come" (4), Jesus did act. He provided, not simply as a favor for his mother or for the bridegroom, but to show how God provides out of concern for human beings.

## "Feel Into" the Text

Relate this story to your own life and congregation. Which character do you identify with most? Mary? Jesus? The bridegroom? The servants? The wine steward? The wedding guests? The disciples? Why? When have you felt inadequate to provide for someone? When have you felt unable to give someone what they needed (material things, love, understanding, knowledge)? What further examples can you think of in which God (seemingly quite miraculously) provided abundantly for you, your family, or your church?

Some Christians struggle with this passage and other stories of signs, wonders, or miracles. What is your attitude toward this story? Do you consider it to be a "tall tale," a folk legend, a slightly exaggerated report, or an unexplained mystery? Critical minds may have difficulty accepting this passage at face value. Human perception is limited by our need for a scientific explanation for everything. One attempt to rationalize this story explained that the jars contained some leftover wine. Adding water to them produced a wine-like mixture. That explanation is far-fetched and irrelevant. Even if we have doubts or questions, we can concede that Jesus did some remarkable things, the significance of which has yet to be fully appreciated or understood. When have you found yourself needing or asking for proofs for your faith? How can we be counted among those whom Jesus was talking about when he said, "Blessed are those who have not seen and yet have come to believe" (John 20:29)?

## In the Midst of the Ordinary, the Miraculous Happens

John tells us that in the midst of everyday, ordinary life, something quietly miraculous has happened. The incredible new life Jesus brings comes to us in ordinary human experience. The Gospel writers often described that new life in terms of the miracles of Jesus. The miracles and signs often took place right there in the middle of daily life, at work, at play, at a wedding. Life goes on, nothing has changed, yet all has changed. How does God bring newness to us in everyday life? How does God work through the events of our lives? How can we receive the transforming power of God? How is new wine manifest in your congregation? How is transformation and newness of life present in the day-to-day operation of your church?

Another important point that is made in this account is that the usual custom or sequence is reversed. Usually, the best wine is used first, but because of Jesus, the best comes last. It is human nature to "want it all" and to want it all at once, right now. Some of us, "kids at heart," eat our dessert before the main course. We want the best, and we want it now. We buy on credit. We are not accustomed to waiting or saving. If we are, however, willing to discipline ourselves in the example of Jesus, to wait, to be good stewards in our use of resources, the lasting rewards are great.

The transformation of water to wine in some ways resembles the life cycle. Life is something good and basic that can become richer with years. Some older persons take the attitude "the best is yet to come." Some have found that despite physical limitations, they are wiser, more knowledgeable, and have more time to "smell the roses." Some cultures honor and revere the aged, acknowledging that the best comes last.

This transformation of water to wine, this first of Jesus' signs that began his public ministry according to John, began the process of uncovering the mystery surrounding the person of Jesus. His disciples looked on in awe, and their faith in him was strengthened. Today, do we look on in critical disbelief or do we look upon this sign in wonder and awe? Can our faith be like that of the disciples, deepened or strengthened by encountering the transforming power of Christ?

## Dimension 4:
## A Daily Bible Journey Plan

*Day 1:* John 3:1-10
*Day 2:* John 3:11-15
*Day 3:* John 3:16-21
*Day 4:* John 3:22-24
*Day 5:* John 3:25-27
*Day 6:* John 3:28-30
*Day 7:* John 3:31-36

# 3

# MORE ENCOUNTERS WITH JESUS

## *What to Watch For*

In chapters 3, 4, and 5 John provides more insight into Jesus by describing encounters between him and Nicodemus, the Samaritan woman, and the paralytic at Bethesda. All three encounters involved conversations with Jesus. These afforded the evangelist the opportunity to expound on the meaning of Jesus' message. This study focuses on the conversation between Jesus and Nicodemus and the discourse that followed. Watch for the following emphases as you read the passage.

➤ Nicodemus, one of the Jewish rulers, came to Jesus perhaps out of curiosity, perhaps out of genuine interest.
➤ John records that Nicodemus failed to understand Jesus when Jesus tried to explain the true nature of faith.
➤ In this passage John tells us that Jesus spoke in a unique way—in a language of heavenly things, of being born from above.
➤ We are told of the incredible love of God. The beloved verse, John 3:16, has been called "the gospel in miniature." It summarizes the message of God's saving action in Christ. You will sense the importance of this text.

1. How did Nicodemus approach Jesus?

2. How did Jesus respond to Nicodemus?

3. How did Jesus and Nicodemus relate to each other?

4. What images did Jesus use to make his point?

5. What were the actions of God as described in this passage?

## Dimension 2:
## What Does the Bible Mean?

In 2:13-25 John discusses Jesus' encounter with the Temple leaders and his challenge of their practices. John then describes Jesus' meeting with one particular leader, Nicodemus. In 2:23-25 John reports that Jesus did not trust those who only believed in him because of his signs. Jesus knew what was in the hearts of those persons. Thus Nicodemus, a character mentioned only in John, came to Jesus in the night. He was a Pharisee, a member of the Sanhedrin, the official Jewish court made up of seventy scribes and elders headed by the high priest. This was the council that eventually handed Jesus over to Pilate and demanded he be crucified.

### A Visit at Night
Nicodemus came at night. Was he sneaking around so that no one would see him? Would he have been ridiculed or endangered if the other members knew of his interest in Jesus? Was it simply a convenient time? John's

mention of darkness could symbolize evil, mystery, or ignorance. Nicodemus may have been shrouded in evil or he may have been "in the dark" about Christ's teachings. However, John's mention of darkness may have merely highlighted a normal event. It was rabbinic custom to stay up late at night to study and discuss the law. Nicodemus may have wanted to speak with Jesus alone and uninterrupted by the crowds that accompanied him during the day.

Nicodemus approached Jesus with an intellectual openness, wanting to engage him in a scholarly debate. He may have been honoring Jesus by addressing him as rabbi, a title of respect, since Jesus was not officially sanctioned as a rabbi. Nicodemus began with a statement, "Rabbi, we know that you are a teacher who has come from God; for no one can do these signs that you do apart from the presence of God" (2). With this Nicodemus threw down the gauntlet, challenging Jesus to respond. He came to Jesus intrigued by his signs, but Jesus' response was not to appease Nicodemus' curiosity by performing another sign. Instead he answered in verse 3, "Very truly, I tell you, no one can see the kingdom of God without being born from above." Persons may "see" signs with their eyes, but according to John's Jesus, unless one is born from above, one cannot "see" or understand or experience or participate in the Kingdom. A mere belief in signs would not suffice. Rather a person's life had to be so dramatically changed by belief that it could only be described as a new birth.

A common device of John was to use words with double meanings. One such phrase was *gennan anothen* in the Greek. It could mean either to be "born again" or to be "born from above." Nicodemus understood Jesus to mean "born again" in the literal sense. He misunderstood Jesus, asking "How can anyone be born after having grown old? Can one enter a second time into the mother's womb and be born? (4) Clearly, Nicodemus was confused. Jesus intended the other meaning of *anothen,* of a higher birth, a birth from the Father. This exchange represented a typical pattern used by John.

## TYPICAL EXCHANGE PATTERN IN JOHN

1. A person met and spoke to Jesus.
2. Jesus responded with something that was difficult to understand.
3. The person misunderstood Jesus.
4. Misunderstanding led to further explanation by Jesus.

Jesus answered Nicodemus' initial confusion. "Very truly, I tell you, no one can enter the kingdom of God without being born of water and Spirit" (5). Jesus contrasted flesh and spirit. The Pharisees thought the kingdom of God was a state built by laws and traditions. Jesus declared that the kingdom of God is from above. To line up signs and proofs is to be of the earth. To receive and accept grace is to be of heaven.

## Born of Water and the Spirit

Water symbolizes cleansing and nourishment. The Spirit is the power and new life that comes from God. To be born of water and the Spirit means to receive God's cleansing grace, to be born from above. Is this a reference to baptism? Scholars debate this point. Nicodemus probably would have known about the baptism of water offered by John the Baptist and, of course, the Jewish rites of purification with water. The evangelist knew about it also, writing when he did. To be born of water and the Spirit was not simply an outward or earthly rite, but inward acceptance of a heavenly grace.

Jesus referred to the wind saying that it blows where it wills, and though we can hear it, we do not know from whence it comes. This is another one of John's play on words. In the Greek, the word *pneuma* is the word for both wind and Spirit. The Spirit is like the wind. It is somewhat mysterious—free to blow where it chooses. It will not be controlled by human laws and dictums. The *sound* of the wind is also the *voice* of the Spirit. It is a voice that calls us, as it called Nicodemus, but we do not know from whence it comes.

Nicodemus did not know either. Jesus grew impatient. "Are you a teacher of Israel, and yet you do not understand these things?" (10) Perhaps Nicodemus should have been able to understand, given his background. The Old Testament had a tradition of being born from above, of water and spirit being connected. See, for example, Ezekiel 36:25-26. Yet this could only take him so far. His knowledge of and adherence to Jewish law failed to provide him with the ultimate truth. Nicodemus' skepticism prevailed. "How can these things be?" (9)

## A Failure to Connect

Nicodemus, an intellectual, sought answers from Jesus, and Jesus provided them. It was not, however, the answer that Nicodemus wanted to hear. He seemed unable or unwilling to accept the truth that Jesus declared. The two failed to connect. The conversation broke down. All was not lost, however, because the conversation provided an opportunity for the evangelist to preach a little. Interestingly, we hear from Nicodemus again, later in the book. In 7:50-52 he defended Jesus to the chief priest and Pharisees, stating that in Jewish law anyone deserves a fair trial. In 19:39 Nicodemus joined with Joseph of Arimathea in taking care of Jesus' body. The Gospel nowhere states that Nicodemus became a follower, but it hints that he came to recognize God's presence in the man Jesus, at least enough to feel that he merited a decent burial.

In the discourse of John 3:11-21 Nicodemus faded into the background, and Jesus began a soliloquy, another literary device of John. Though the speaker was Jesus, it is apparent that the writer intended to speak to his readers through Jesus.

## LITERARY DEVICES COMMON IN JOHN

- Use of words with double meanings;
- Use of the motif of misunderstanding as a means of further explanation;
- soliloquy or discourse directed at the audience (as in *Hamlet*);
- use of contrasting themes including flesh/spirit, earth/heaven, light/dark.

In verse 11 John had Jesus use the plural "we." Who is *we*? Jesus and God? Jesus and the disciples? Other followers in contrast with the Jews? It is unclear just who is meant by the pronoun, but John seemed intent on giving the conversation more significance than one occurring between two people. John may have attempted to give more authority to Jesus on the rationale that speaking in the plural would carry more weight. Regardless, the debate quickly shifted from Jesus and Nicodemus to a debate between the church and the synagogue.

Jesus contrasted earthly things and heavenly things in verse 12. This is not a dualism of good and bad, but a contrast of two kinds of divine action. Jesus spoke to those who did not accept what he said and did. He knew they would certainly not be able to believe when he spoke of mysterious heavenly things. The writer in verse 13 seemed to know that Jesus was ascended. Some scholars believe that the writer of this Gospel, or a later editor who knew about the Ascension, was looking back on Jesus' life and added this detail for emphasis. The verse could also be saying that no one else had been with God to know of heavenly things and then descended to earth as did Jesus.

### God So Loved the World

Jesus, a doer of signs, chose to use a sign of Moses to harness the attention of the Jews. Moses was greatly revered by the Jews. Jesus referred to Numbers 21:4-9. Out in the wilderness the Israelites complained and wanted to turn back, and so God sent fiery serpents. God also provided a way to save them through Moses. Moses lifted up a bronze serpent on a pole, as instructed by God, so that when the wounded and dead looked upon it, they would be healed and live. In the same way, Jesus ultimately was lifted up, exalted, believed in, and looked upon in faith. Jesus became the source of healing and salvation. In the wilderness ancient people had looked on the serpent, which was like turning one's glance toward God. In the Crucifixion the attention of the world would turn toward Golgotha.

Believing on Jesus in this way brings eternal life. John 3:16 states it as eloquently as any statement ever written. God sent his Son into the world. Word was made flesh. God loved the world. This action was love. God loved not just a few Christians; God loved the world. The Son was sent not to condemn the world, not to say no to the world, but to say yes. God sent the light, but the light exposes human blemishes. Many prefer to live in darkness, as Nicodemus, who furtively approached and departed in the night. Those who live in truth, however, those who "do truth," and want to know truth, and accept the truth of Jesus Christ come into the light and see clearly.

## Dimension 3:
## What Does the Bible Mean to Us?

### Faith Seeking Understanding

In John's Gospel we meet a lot of puzzled characters. The wine steward was puzzled about where the new wine came from. Nicodemus was confused and misunderstood Jesus. The Samaritan woman wondered aloud about the origin of living water. Actually, the characters in John's Gospel were puzzled about the origin and meaning of Jesus himself.

The puzzlement and confusion of these biblical characters is not unlike the ambivalence many have toward Christianity today. Who among even the staunchest of believers has not been confused about Christianity or the meaning of Christ at one time or another? We may not understand certain aspects, certain doctrines, or biblical passages. Our uncertainty may bother us; it may be quite uncomfortable. Occasionally such perplexity is so painful that people give up trying. More often though, the confusion leads one to a stronger, deeper faith. The confusion motivates us to learn more, to become seekers after truth. Our faith is as St. Anselm described it—*credo ut intelligum*—faith seeking understanding.

### Faith Seeking Commitment

It is possible that one might understand Nicodemus as a hypocrite, coming to Jesus in the night, ashamed to be seen, baiting Jesus with slick talk. Another way of looking at him is as a seeker after the truth. Many people first come to Christ as seekers "in the night." Sometimes persons become curious and approach Christianity very cautiously. There comes a point, however, when one has to shake off the fear that prevents one from full commitment.

Jesus was trying to tell Nicodemus just that. The fear and hostility of the Jewish rulers toward Jesus blinded them to the truth. Christians today sometimes feel that same fear, shame, and embarrassment about their faith. Many of us only approach Jesus when no one is looking. Yet Jesus calls us to come out into the light of day and live the truth. To do that requires a complete turn toward God.

Jesus said that conversion was like being born from above. We are all born of earthly parents, but Christians must have a parent in heaven. The phrase "born from above" or "born again," as it is often translated, has been misconstrued. We read about persons who describe themselves as "born-again Christians" as if this were an earned title conveyed upon an exclusive few. Soon the novelty wears off. Some Christians do experience an all-at-once conversion to Christ. Many describe such conversion as being "born again." Others experience a more gradual turning toward God, which though different from the sudden conversion, is also a legitimate conversion or way of being "born again." What is the difference?

The difference has been compared to two different ways used to break a horse. One method is to break the horse in one afternoon by relentless effort. Another method is to train the horse gradually, starting by getting the horse used to the bit one day. The next day the trainer may get the horse used to the saddle. Later, the trainer will attempt to mount. Eventually the horse is broken.

Coming to Christ is not primarily something human beings do. Men and women can come to Christ only as that possibility has been provided through God's initiative.

Jesus did not elaborate on how one is born anew, only that one must become a son or daughter of God. He did say that becoming a child of God involved a full commitment. There can be no subterfuge or "sneaking around" in the night. One must fully and completely turn to God. As ancient people turned and looked upon the serpent in the wilderness, we must turn our hearts toward Jesus and believe on him.

## God Struggles With Us

Nicodemus did not seem all that evil. He appeared rather harmless, if maybe a little spineless. For such a learned scholar, as he was supposed to be, he seemed a little dense! Jesus, however, was distrustful of the motives of Nicodemus. Jesus did not intend for persons to be impressed with him because of his signs. Like many people today Nicodemus wanted to believe for all the wrong reasons. Like Nicodemus many of us think that accepting Jesus will solve all our problems or give us some magical means of controlling life. God does not treat us as puppets, solving all our problems and struggles; God struggles with us.

Jesus answered Nicodemus respectfully, but Nicodemus was not satisfied. He could not comprehend. Like many persons today, he was more comfortable with his old ways than with something new. Nicodemus was not ready or able to grasp the truth of which Jesus spoke. Isn't it sometimes easier to obey laws, rules, and dictums than to accept and live in grace?

Christians reading this portion of John should not give up on Nicodemus.

There is some evidence that he may have grown in his ability to accept Jesus. When he appears again in John, he seems to have a different attitude toward Jesus. He participated in the loving and courageous act of removing Jesus' body from the scene at Golgotha when most of Jesus' followers had already fled the scene.

## Responding to God's Love

Throughout the Gospels one can find the stories of persons who encountered Jesus who were at different stages in their faith maturity. Nicodemus was captivated by the signs performed by Jesus. It was a literal, initial seed of faith that perhaps grew. John depicted faith as dynamic—capable of growing and developing. Everyone who decided to follow Jesus had to continue to affirm that decision again and again. Some were not able to do so and abandoned him. Today, some still do.

To be born of water and the Spirit is to turn to and accept Jesus, to be washed over by God's cleansing love, and to commit to the truth of God in Christ. It is to commit one's life to seeking God by the power of the Spirit, even in moments of doubt.

The Christian practice of baptism expresses this commitment. John summed it up for us: "For God so loved the world that he gave his only Son, so that everyone who believes in him may not perish but may have eternal life" (16). To fail to believe is to perish, to live apart from God, to live a dead, meaningless life, and to experience the consequences of being separated from God. God does not want us to perish. The purpose of sending Jesus on a mission was not condemnation but salvation. Acting in love, God has gone to the ultimate lengths for us. John wants us, his readers, to know this and respond accordingly. It is his critical, urgent message.

## *Dimension 4:*
## *A Daily Bible Journey Plan*

*Day 1:* **John 4:1-15**
*Day 2:* **John 4:16-26**
*Day 3:* **John 4:27-42**
*Day 4:* **John 4:43-54**
*Day 5:* **John 5:1-18**
*Day 6:* **John 5:19-30**
*Day 7:* **John 5:31-47**

**John
6:22-71**

# NOURISHMENT

## *What to Watch For*

Jesus described himself as the Bread of Life and expounded upon the meaning of that for the crowds that followed him to Capernaum. John 6:22-71 is a lengthy passage with rich material to be studied and savored. Watch for the following emphases as you read.

➤ Note that the context is just after the sign of the feeding of the five thousand. A crowd followed him clamoring for more bread. They were looking for more manna like that which was provided in the wilderness for the early Jews escaping Egypt.

➤ Jesus explained that what he offered was not physical bread, but spiritual nourishment. In language that sounds very sacramental, Jesus told of the life his followers could receive in partaking in him.

➤ God sent Jesus to bring eternal life. Many in the crowd could not accept this idea and "murmered against him" and left him. Only the Twelve remained, but even one of them would betray him.

➤ This occasion for more teaching about Jesus already foreshadows the beginning of the end.

1. Why did the people cross the sea to Capernaum?

2. What did the people ask Jesus when they found him, and what was Jesus' reply?

3. What is this food that gives eternal life?

4. How did the crowd respond to Jesus' teaching?

5. What was the "hard saying" of Jesus?

6. What did Jesus ask the Twelve?

## Dimension 2:
## What Does the Bible Mean?

### The Crowds Sought Jesus

Chapter 6 opens with the story of the miraculous feeding of the five thousand by the Sea of Galilee at Passover time. The Sea of Galilee was also called the Sea of Tiberias, particularly after the first century. It was so named for the city of Tiberias on the west side of the lake (see map, inside back cover). The people were so impressed by the miracle that they wanted to make Jesus king, but he retreated to a mountain. He returned and mysteriously walked on the sea to calm the disciples caught in a squall. He got in the disciple's boat and went with them where they were going.

The crowd lingered by the lake, waiting for Jesus. They expected that he was around somewhere, because there was only one boat, and the disciples left in it without Jesus. They had not seen him join them on the lake.

Some boats began to come from the city of Tiberias into the bay. Realizing that they had missed Jesus, the crowds sailed for Capernaum to look for Jesus. Capernaum was a city on the northwest shore of the Sea of Galilee, and a center of Jesus' ministry (see map, inside back cover). True to expectations, Jesus was in Capernaum when the crowds arrived.

## The Crowds Complained

The crowd began to "murmur" against Jesus. Clamoring for more bread, the people sought Jesus. Once again they misunderstood Jesus and his actions. They thought Jesus had provided bread to save them from hunger. They perceived it to be a "sign," a miracle of compassion. They sought Jesus because they saw in him someone who could meet their physical needs. Jesus explained that he meant the providing of bread as a sign that he was the bread of life, the source of true nourishment. John did not focus on this sign of the feeding of the multitude as an act of compassion or a mere display of power (just as he did not focus on the sign at Cana as such). The evangelist saw these events as truly miraculous but interpreted them as having a significance beyond the miraculous.

The phrase, "very truly, I tell you," reveals that John perceived that what Jesus was about to say was the precise, true message of God. In verse 27 Jesus claimed that the Son of man would give eternal nourishment. God had set a seal on him.

### God's Seal

In ancient Palestine a seal was made of clay or metal and was used to emboss or imprint a document to make it authentic and valid. A seal made something or someone authoritative, in much the same way that today a notary public notarizes or makes authoritative a signature or document. God's seal was on Jesus as the Son of man ensuring that he was God's agent bearing the message of truth.

## Jesus Told the Crowds to Believe

The people asked (in verses 28-29) what works they could do in order to please God and receive God's nourishment. Instead of giving them a list of things to do, Jesus told them they must believe. That work was all they had to do, the work of faith. In believing, they entered into a relationship with God.

The crowd told Jesus that their ancestors had been provided with bread from heaven when they were in the wilderness. They expected him to likewise provide such bread. (See Exodus 16.) Yet Jesus had just fed five thousand people from five barley loaves and two fish! What more could they want?

There was a strong rabbinic tradition that when the Messiah came, he would bring manna again like that which had been given in the wilderness (Numbers 11:8; Psalm 78:24; Revelation 2:17). Jesus had taken real bread and multiplied it. They asked him to produce bread from heaven that would feed the people like Moses had done. The Jews expected the Messiah to be a great leader of Israel like Moses.

The people wanted further evidence that Jesus was the second Moses. Jesus answered them that it was not Moses who gave the manna, but God, and that it was not physical food that was needed, but spiritual food. Manna was perishable. It was merely a symbol of a more enduring food, the bread of life (35). The bread provided in the feeding of the multitude, like the manna, though supernatural, only lasted for a day. Jesus as the bread of life would last for eternity.

The crowd's interest was piqued. Everyone would love never-ending bread! "Give us this bread always," they asked in verse 34. Just as the Samaritan woman wanted living water in John 4:15, they wanted bread that would give them life forever. Jesus, however, did not offer physical immortality.

Jesus' statement, "I am the bread of life," was made against the background of the Old Testament. John had Jesus use the term twenty-six times. There are seven very familiar "I am" (*ego eimi*) statements where Jesus used a descriptive word to follow the "I am." Exodus 3:14 is the backdrop. Jesus was not claiming to be God by the use of this term, but he was claiming to be sent from God.

> Jesus' words were associated with Jewish writings such as Deuteronomy 8:3 that "man does not live by bread alone." Matthew and Luke also recorded that Jesus quoted this tradition to them (Matthew 4:4; Luke 4:4) when he was tempted by the devil in the wilderness.

---

## *I AM* STATEMENTS IN JOHN

- I am the bread of life (6:35)
- I am the light of the world (8:12)
- I am the gate for the sheep (10:7)
- I am the good shepherd (10:11)
- I am the resurrection and the life (11:25)
- I am the way, and the truth, and the life (14:6)
- I am the true vine (15:1)

---

Verses 37-40 and 44 refer to the last days. Jesus is God's gift. Why some believe and others do not is a mystery, but no one who seeks Jesus is rejected (37). Those who do believe in Jesus will be kept by the Son until the consummation of the resurrection at the last days. To believe in Jesus means to enter into and possess eternal life now and hope for resurrection at the last day.

All this talk displeased the crowd and drove them to "murmuring" as the Israelites murmured in the wilderness (Exodus 16:2). Verses 41-42 show that some of these people rejected Jesus and his claim to be the bread from heaven because they knew him to be of humble origins and considered there was nothing special about him. They judged him by externals. He appeared to be a mere carpenter's son.

## God Draws People

Jesus talked about how God would "draw" people unto him. The Jews began arguing about what Jesus was saying. Some simply walked away. Jesus spoke of eating the flesh of the Son of man and drinking his blood as a requirement for believing and having life. This talk sounds like he is referring to the Lord's Supper, which was not started until the night before Jesus died, according to tradition. John did not record it. It has been suggested that since John, or others who edited the material, knew about the Lord's Supper, they may have put this "spin" on this teaching of Jesus. Or, possibly Jesus anticipated what was to come. Jesus may or may not have been speaking directly of the Lord's Supper, but what he said does contribute to the understanding of it. He expounded on a truth that is conveyed in the Lord's Supper.

> The word for *draw* is the word that is also used in the Bible for drawing in a net full of fish or for drawing one's sword. It implies some resistance. It is the word used in Jeremiah 31:3, "With loving kindness have I drawn thee." The word is *helkuein*. God pulls at people. God's intent is to rein human beings in, much as fish are drawn into a heavily laden net. Many are drawn in. Through teaching and hearing God's word people are brought to Christ. However, one must never make the assumption that all will indeed be drawn in. Fish escape the fish net. People refuse the pull of God.

## A Hard Saying

For the disciples who heard, it was a "hard saying." (The word *disciples* here loosely refers to the crowd of followers.) It was a hard saying in that it was certainly offensive to Jews to eat flesh and drink blood (Genesis 9:4; Leviticus 3:17). Even if they knew that Jesus was speaking figuratively, it was still hard to accept. Jesus insisted that he did not offer some abstract ideology to adhere to, but one had to adhere to him. He offered himself. The words of the Communion liturgy express it, "Feed on him in your heart with thanksgiving." Flesh and blood may be offensive, but even more offensive and harder to take is Christ's free offer of himself—undeserved, unearned grace.

Many of his followers defected. Jesus questioned the Twelve about their loyalty. This was John's only mention of the Twelve as such. He must have assumed that his readers would already know about their selection because he did not record anything about the selection. Peter was the spokesperson. He professed loyalty and belief. Peter called Jesus the "Holy One of God," a messianic title also used in Mark 1:24 and Luke 4:34 by a demon-possessed person. This profession parallels one made in Caesarea Philippi recorded in Mark 8:27-30 and Matthew 16:13-20. Yet there was one among the Twelve whom Jesus pointed out. This person would fail to believe and ally with the Devil to become an adversary of God. John identified the one as Judas and then left this discussion moving on to other occasions on which to teach about Jesus.

## Dimension 3:
## What Does the Bible Mean to Us?

The crowds clamored for Jesus. He could provide bread like Moses did. He could provide an unending source of life. Having enough food was a great concern among most of the population in ancient times. Planning for and gathering food consumed much of their waking hours and a great deal of effort. The people clamored for Jesus because they saw him provide this food.

### Spiritual Hunger Marks Our Lives

People today also clamor for Jesus, for his word and the life he brings. We want to be filled. We long for and crave such spiritual nourishment. Too often what we settle for is "junk food" to temporarily abate the hunger. We seek nourishment from the wrong places, places that can only provide another theory, another program, another quick fix. We run through a smorgasbord of options testing out shallow gimmicks or causes tossed to and fro by whim. We consume an unbalanced diet that leaves us feeling stuffed, not nourished. There is a spiritual hunger that physical things can never satisfy. Sometimes we try to fill this hunger, this empty void, with material things; but somehow these do not satisfy. It is still a profound question for us today: Why do we spend so much time, effort, and energy on that which is perishable?

Often we hear or read of those who "have it all": success, money, a big house, a nice car, a perfect family, yet they resort to drastic or destructive measures because they are not satisfied. They have all the external trappings of happiness, yet inside are spiritually dead. The truth is that these people are not just people we read about; we are these people. We live in a time of spiritual famine, even in the midst of plenty.

## Jesus Still Nourishes

In this text we again have the problem raised that there are those who follow Jesus because of his signs, his powers, or what he can provide. As in the wedding at Cana and with Nicodemus, this reason for looking to Jesus is inadequate. Admittedly, Jesus does do signs, and yes, he does provide; but that is not the reason we should seek him, nor should our only experience of Jesus be asking him to provide. We can seek Jesus not just for things, not just for physical nourishment, but we can seek him for himself, to know him, to believe in him.

This spiritual hunger cannot be "fed" by going to church once or twice a year, or just by attending church solely out of habit. Spiritual hunger is never-ending in this life. Just like we have to eat every day, we constantly have to partake of the bread of life.

Not only did many of the Jewish opponents of Jesus reject Jesus, but most of the crowds, the initial followers of Jesus, abandoned him as well. They went on to place their hopes on other causes or leaders. So-called Christians today still abandon him because they find his sayings too hard, the Christian life too demanding.

Just as the crowd murmured against Jesus' teaching, so do we. We do not like it because it is hard. It is hard to continually seek and "partake" of Jesus. We are called to an intimate relationship, to lose ourselves in him; but our egos tell us we can make it on our own. The crowd asked for Jesus' résumé. They wanted to know his credentials for claiming to be greater than Moses. It is a difficult concept to accept that nothing we can do—no credentials, no achievements, no number of earned degrees, no amount of financial success—can make one any closer to God. Only in Jesus can we really live. Only in him is eternal life. We can easily enough hear what is involved in believing in Jesus. And even the most intelligent persons among us may know "in our heads" what it takes and still have great difficulty accepting grace and living by it. The nourishment of our spiritual life comes by feeding on Christ, through praying, hearing, and studying the Word, and by coming to the Holy Table.

## None Will Be Rejected

In this passage, that spiritual hunger or longing is described beautifully as God drawing us, pulling us, toward him. Yet we do have free choice. We have the ability to resist, and we often do. In fact, as said above, it is easy to resist. What is hardest is to "let go" and accept Christ. God does not control our lives by drawing us into Christ. Our lives are not predetermined. God does not choose a select few. All are given the opportunity to believe, states John. No one who comes will be rejected.

What is so difficult to accept and understand is that God is the initiator of salvation. We do not and can not know why some believe and others do

not. It is God who saves through Jesus. The name *Jesus* actually means
"God saves."

The failure to believe is not just a problem of persons from other religious traditions. It affects supposed followers of Jesus as well. Even the
inner circle of the twelve persons closest to Jesus was not immune. One would reject him totally, others doubted him or denied him.

Jesus was involved in an argument over the nature of faith. The Jews had one understanding of faith, Jesus proposed another. It caused great debate and bitter controversy. In the Gospel of John there emerged a sense of what true faith consisted of: receiving undeserved grace and believing in Jesus. Some opposed it because of their presuppositions.

The question of faith is still relevant. Are we ready to accept what is required of true faith? Are we ready to accept God's love? Are we ready to do the one true work of God? When someone or something comes along offering a quick fix, an easy out, temporary nourishment, are we tempted to jump on the bandwagon and snap it up quickly? Or are we willing to take the road less traveled, to accept the hard sayings? To do so is to abide in Christ and he in us.

> What is so difficult to accept and understand is that God is the initiator of salvation. We do not and can not know why some believe and others do not. It is God who saves through Jesus. The name *Jesus* actually means "God saves."

## Dimension 4:
## A Daily Bible Journey Plan

*Day 1:*  **John 6:1-15**

*Day 2:*  **John 6:16-21**

*Day 3:*  **John 6:22-27**

*Day 4:*  **John 6:28-34**

*Day 5:*  **John 6:35-40**

*Day 6:*  **John 6:41-51**

*Day 7:*  **John 6:52-71**

**John
7:37-39;
8:12-20**

# 5

# WATER AND LIGHT

## What to Watch For

Against the background of the Jewish Festival of Tabernacles or Booths, one of the three great celebrations of the Jewish year, Jesus made some significant pronouncements. As you read, watch for these particular emphases:

➤ At the Feast of Tabernacles Jesus proclaimed, "Let anyone who is thirsty come to me, and let the one who believes in me drink" (37-38). He spoke of "rivers of living water" (38).

➤ John states that the ever-flowing stream was the Spirit that would come to believers when Jesus was glorified (39).

➤ The crowd was in great disagreement over Jesus' words. Some officers were sent to arrest Jesus but went back to the Pharisees without him, apparently both enthralled and confused.

➤ Jesus continued to teach in the Temple calling himself "the light of the world" (8:12). Many who heard thought him to be arrogant and his self-given title a blatant breach of the law. They challenged Jesus' testimony on behalf of himself, but Jesus declared his relationship with God and told how God had sent him to bear witness to the truth.

➤ Water and light are two things that are absolutely necessary for life. John's claim in this text is that Jesus is just as indispensable.

## Dimension 1:
## What Does the Bible Say?

1. What did Jesus stand up and say on the last day of the feast?

2. What was John's explanation?

3. When Jesus described himself as the light of the world, what was the Pharisees' response?

4. Who did Jesus declare to be his other witness?

## Dimension 2:
## What Does the Bible Mean?

### The Greatest of the Feasts

John tells his readers as chapter 7 opens that Jesus focused his ministry in Galilee seeking to avoid those in Judea who sought to kill him. His was a dangerous mission. In 7:10 Jesus left Galilee and returned to Jerusalem for the Feast of Tabernacles, also known as Sukkoth or "ingathering." It was probably the earliest and greatest of the feasts (Leviticus 23:33-43; Deuteronomy 16:13-15).

---

## MAJOR JEWISH FEASTS

**Passover** (Feast of Unleavened Bread)—See John 2:23; 6:4; 11:55; 13:1

**Pentecost** (Feast of Weeks)—Occurs seven weeks after Passover

**Feast of Tabernacles** (Feast of Booths)—See John 7:2; 7:14; 7:37

**Hanukkah** (Feast of Dedication)—See John 10:22

---

37

It was customary for Jews to make a pilgrimage to Jerusalem for the feasts. In 7:1-13 Jesus' brothers challenged him to do his work out in the open. Why?

Perhaps they wanted Jesus to "get on with it"—to confirm to his followers that he was who he said he was. Perhaps the brothers were jesting—poking fun as it were. After all, they did not appear to believe fully in Jesus themselves. They may have been taunting Jesus to go to Judea as a test of his strength. While many human beings would have accepted the challenge, traveling to Jerusalem as one of the teeming crowds and seeking recognition through a public display of power, Jesus chose not to accept his brothers' challenge. The Scriptures are clear. Jesus was not swayed by human opinion, but acted in ways consistent with God's desires. In this case, as indicated in verse 8, his hour had not yet fully come.

## Jesus Came in Secret

When Jesus did sense it was time to go, he went in private, not with the usual crowds (10). Some people had come to Jerusalem, hoping to catch a glimpse of Jesus. There was much muttering about him among the pilgrims, with probably a good bit of debate regarding Jesus' character. At some point during the feast Jesus went to the Temple (14), according to John, and taught openly. Those who heard him marveled at Jesus' teachings and asked how someone who had not studied formally could show such wisdom. Jesus told them that his teaching came from God, adding "Those who speak on their own seek their own glory; but the one who seeks the glory of him who sent him is true, and there is nothing false in him" (18).

It is at this point that Jesus referred to the reason he had centered his ministry in Galilee. He chastised those who had gathered to hear him in the Temple for trying to rely on the law. It is important to remember the site for this particular debate as well as the probable audience. Jesus stood in the midst of the Temple! He spoke not only to the masses of pilgrims who came to celebrate the festival (and who did not fully understand that their religious leaders wanted to kill Jesus) but also to the religious authorities!

This is the audience to whom Jesus declared that it was hypocrisy to want to kill him for healing on the sabbath when they circumcised on the sabbath. The law said to do no work on the sabbath, but it also said to circumcise a child when he is eight days old. Those who interpreted the law decided that if the eighth day fell on a sabbath, then circumcision still should be done. Jesus maintained that if circumcision was permitted, so was healing. The law provided that human needs be met wherever and whenever they occurred. Elsewhere Jesus was recorded to have said, "The sabbath was made for humankind, and not humankind for the sabbath" (Mark 2:27).

## The Crowd Was Divided

Jesus' teaching caused division among the crowds. Some were convinced he was the expected Messiah. Some wanted him killed. Yet, as John noted, he was allowed to teach publicly. Perhaps those who opposed him lacked enough "on him" yet. The muttering continued, and the priests and Pharisees sent officers to arrest Jesus, but he held them off by telling them that he would be leaving soon (32-33). Jesus said he would be going back to the one who sent him.

Understandably, those who heard Jesus did not understand his statements. Questioning one another they asked, "Where does this man intend to go that we will not find him?" (35) They questioned if Jesus was going out to teach the Jews of the Dispersion (those who lived among the Gentiles).

## The Last Day of the Feast

The last day of the feast came (37), the greatest day; a day of celebration. It was the custom on each of the seven days of the feast for the Jews to carry a pitcher of water from the Pool of Siloam at the bottom of the hill up to the Temple. This pool is where the healing in chapter 9 took place. Each morning a procession went up from the pool. Pilgrims carried *lulabs* (branches) of myrtle, willow, and palm to the altar. The people recited Isaiah 12:3, "With joy you will draw water from the wells of salvation." The priests, after walking around the altar, poured the water through a silver funnel onto the ground.

It was a ritual of thanksgiving for a good harvest and a prayer for rains to ensure a good crop for the following year. All of this was the context for Jesus' words, "Let anyone who is thirsty come to me, and let the one who believes in me drink" (37-38). It was an invitation to believe—to have at one's disposal a spring, a river of constantly flowing, life-giving water.

This section continues with an exploration of the division of opinion about Jesus. The people began to debate about whether he was a prophet (a messianic forerunner) or the Christ (the Messiah). Some wanted him arrested. When the officers sent to arrest him (7:32) returned without him (verse 45), the Pharisees demanded to know why. The officers confessed they were both intrigued and impressed by Jesus' speaking ability. The Pharisees asked if they were going over to his side, pointing out their own negative conclusions about Jesus. Nicodemus, whom we have already encountered, defended Jesus' right to fair judgment (51). In so doing, he brought recrimination upon himself.

# CONSIDER SOME QUESTIONS

There are two questions associated with John 7:37-39. First, what Scripture was Jesus quoting? The quotation in verse 38 does not appear in that form in the Bible in spite of the remark "as the scripture has said." However, it is the same idea that is present in Isaiah 44:3, Isaiah 55:1, Psalm 78:16, and Zechariah 14:8. This passage may pick up themes from the vision of Zechariah of the triumphant day of the Lord. Another possible background for the quote is the rock that Moses struck in the wilderness, which produced a stream of water described in Exodus 17. This would certainly fit in with other references John made to the Exodus. (Some of these passages may have been read during the Feast of Tabernacles. A prominent image of God's abode was the river of life described in Psalm 46:4, Ezekiel 47:1-2, and Revelation 22:1.)

A second question is, Do the rivers of living water flow out of Jesus' heart or out of the believer's heart? Which way should the passage be interpreted? Some scholars say the source of the water is Jesus and cite passages that would confirm this viewpoint, such as John 4:10 and 19:34 (where water flowed from Jesus' side). Others believe the source of the spring is the believer and cite many authorities who grant this interpretation. Still others say the source is God and point to the Old Testament image of the river of life flowing from the throne of God.

The writer makes an editorial comment that the water is a symbol of the Spirit and that Jesus was talking about the Spirit, even though the Spirit (as experienced at Pentecost) had not yet been given. He was not intending to say that the Spirit did not exist before the time of Jesus. The Spirit had not been completely given in all its fullness until Jesus was glorified. John wished to convey that Jesus taught how the Spirit was communicated through him and would operate in a way that was not previously possible.

## I Am the Light of the World

Chapter 8 opens with the scribes bringing the woman accused of adultery to Jesus. This text showed Jesus' great compassion for sinners and the forgiveness he offered. It also underscored that the religious authorities were building a case against Jesus, consistently testing Jesus' understanding of the law and his willingness to live within it.

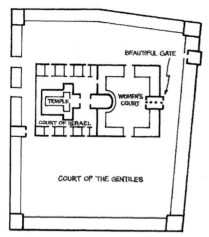

**BEAUTIFUL GATE**

**TEMPLE**

**WOMEN'S COURT**

**COURT OF ISRAEL**

**COURT OF THE GENTILES**

John 8:12-20 continues along the same lines as 7:37-39. Jesus was teaching in the treasury (8:20)—a storage chamber or kind of porch around the Court of Women where treasure chests were kept for people to place their offerings.

On the first night of the festival a ceremony called the "Illumination of the Temple" was held. Four candelabra were lit in the Court of Women. It was said to illuminate all of Jerusalem. This dramatic ritual re-enacted how God led Israel out of the wilderness with a pillar of fire by night (Exodus 13:21). Jesus declared that he was "the light of the world" (12). That God would send light to the world was a theme apparent in Old Testament prophecy (Isaiah 9:1-2; 60:1-3).

The Pharisees were hostile to Jesus' claim because the Messiah was expected to bring God's light into the world. With this claim Jesus identified himself as that Messiah. The Pharisees argued a point of law: that testimony about oneself is not valid. (See Deuteronomy 19:15, 17:6, and Numbers 35:30, which state that more than one witness is required to make a valid testimony.) While affirming the law, Jesus maintained the truth in what he said, because he knew of where he had come and of where he was going. In John 8:17 Jesus referred to the law as "your law" as if he were disassociating himself from it. Yet John showed that Jesus took Jewish law very seriously and considered it binding. He knew the law and tried to comply with it.

He did this, first, by pointing out the error of judging by externals (6:42). Jesus' intention was not to judge or condemn, but to save. When the Pharisees confronted Jesus regarding his testimony, Jesus named himself and God as witnesses. "Where is your Father?" they asked (19). Jesus replied that if they knew him, they would

In the bitter exchange of John 8, Jesus was accused of egotism and arrogance (13), of being suicidal (22), possibly of being illegitimate (19, 41), of being insane or possessing a demon (48, 52). Jesus did not allow himself to be run over here. He told his accusers frankly that they lacked true knowledge of God (19, 55) and that they were dying in sin (21). In what must have seemed to be supreme arrogance he told them, "I tell you, before Abraham was, I am" (58). The chapter ends with an attempt to stone him.

41

know God. Although his answer appeared arrogant to those who battled him, Jesus was not being arrogant. He simply knew his authority was from God.

## Dimension 3:
## What Does the Bible Mean to Us?

### Expressing the Extraordinary

A woman came to consciousness after lengthy surgery in the recovery unit of the hospital. The first thought, the first sensation, she felt was an incredible thirst—a dry, dusty, parched mouth, a need for water that penetrated every ounce of her being. That is how she knew she was alive—that she had made it through the surgery—she later recalled. She drank deeply from a cup with a straw that the nurse gave her. Never before had she experienced such relief!

There is an increasing lack of appreciation for symbols in our modern, technological world. Humans need such symbols as water and light. It would be difficult to express our faith without them. Water and light join the symbol of bread, discussed in the previous chapter, as ordinary things that express the extraordinary.

The late scientist Loren Eisley once stated in his book, *The Immense Journey* (Vintage, 1957; page 15) that "if there is magic on this planet, it is contained in water."

Take water, for example. Water satisfies thirst. Water cleanses. It generates power; it even heals. Many of us are attracted to a quiet lake or a pretty stream, a dazzling waterfall or a majestic ocean. Some travel miles to experience the healing powers of certain springs. With increasing pollution in our world, there is a new appreciation for clean, pure water. In short, without water we could not live. What a powerful and appropriate symbol to use in speaking of Jesus!

On that day long ago, the people had walked for miles to come to the feast. The pilgrims came to pray for rain. Their prayers for water were answered unexpectedly in Jesus. In much the same way we all come to Jesus, even today. We are pilgrims in our faith, searching for something. In him we find the living water, a wellspring of blessing.

We can all partake of the living water. Curiously we are reluctant. "What's the catch?" say our suspicious minds. "What will I have to do? Will I have to serve on a committee?" Sometimes we fall into the trap of those who analyze the water so much (like many of those who opposed Jesus and tried to find something wrong with it) that we don't take the time to drink.

John's message is that Christian believers are given the living water in the Spirit. What differences does this living water make in our own lives?

42

How do we experience the living water? What does the living water do for us? It is difficult to describe. Without Christ in our lives we are just dust, dried up, dead. With Christ we have a perpetual source that quenches the soul. This idea is certainly not to imply that the Christian life is easy. One senses the difficulty in the conflict between Jesus and his listeners. This text provides some vital teachings for us. Our own reaction to them may be as varied as the Jews. Some teachings may be nearly as difficult for us to accept.

## What Stands in the Way of Ministry?

What was Jesus saying that so incited the crowds? Jesus confronted the Jewish use of the law that was being used against him as a weapon. Legalism was blinding the Jewish leaders to human need. Jesus respected the law. He tried to provide the necessary witnesses. He taught, however, that the law can be misused. The Jews were torn between intrigue with Jesus and faithfulness to the law that they had been taught to keep in tact at all costs. Their's was a difficult dilemma not unlike our own struggle with doing what our Christian faith demands, even though it may be in conflict with other expectations. We are subject to such legalism in our communities, jobs, and churches today. Jesus taught that we should move deeper to the heart of the matter. Have we too often failed to answer a human need because it was impractical, not customary, or required us to change? Have we let an opportunity to serve pass us by because we thought it might create problems? Do we let tradition, rules, and bureaucracy stand in the way of our ministry? We do need order, structure, and rules in our lives. Jesus was not out to do away with the law. His presence, love, and grace washes over us as living water, giving us new life and hope.

Jesus confronted his accusers for judging by appearances. The story about the woman caught in adultery in 8:1-11 is a case in point. The woman was a sinner, an adulteress. Jesus refused to condemn her. Instead he forgave her.

It is human nature to "judge a book by its cover." First impressions are often long-lasting! Do we misjudge others in our impetuousness? Do we judge people on the basis of their age, gender, occupation, or ethnic background? Christianity is more about compassion than condemnation. Can we accept and live by this teaching of Jesus?

## Jesus Illumines the Christian Journey

Jesus declared to his accusers that he was "the light of the world." Light is one of the most studied, the most respected, the most mysterious of scientific phenomena. Some of its properties are known, yet some are difficult to grasp. Light is a form of energy that travels at a speed of about 186,300 miles a second. To somewhat oversimplify, in physics there are two schools of thought that attempt to explain light: the wave theory and the particle theory. There is truth in both of these theories, yet scientists acknowledge that light is much more than can be described by theory. There is something mysterious about it, something not quite graspable. Perhaps this is why light is a good way to express the presence of Christ.

Jesus is moral, intellectual, and spiritual light for us. He is the light that shines on injustice and leads us to do good. He is the light that enlightens our minds, that frees us from ignorance, and helps us know truth. He is the light that illumines the Christian journey.

Where there is light, there is also shadow. Humans seem to flounder and struggle in darkness, preferring evil to good, ignorance to knowledge. Darkness does not just penetrate the alleyways of the ghetto. Evil does not exist only in other people. It is a threatening presence in all our lives in the form of close-mindedness, intolerance, indifference, self-satisfaction, and bitterness. The good news is that Jesus is the light. The light of Christ cannot be contained but shines forth into all the world.

## Dimension 4:
## A Daily Bible Journey Plan

*Day 1:* **John 7:1-36**

*Day 2:* **John 7:37-52**

*Day 3:* **John 7:53–8:47**

*Day 4:* **John 8:48-59**

*Day 5:* **John 9:1-12**

*Day 6:* **John 9:13-34**

*Day 7:* **John 9:35-41**

# 6

# THE GOOD SHEPHERD

## *What to Watch For*

Picture the weather-beaten shepherd out on the craggy, plateau country of
Palestine—afraid to sleep, standing by, keeping vigil over the sheep.
Come what may, wolves or storms or thieves, the shepherd is diligent. In
John 10:1-18 Jesus contrasted the true shepherd who knows and cares for
his sheep with imposters and deceitful bandits. He went on to describe
himself as the gate of the sheepfold, the entryway to an eternal relationship with God. As you read this passage, watch for these emphases:

➤ In order to close the gap between first-century Palestine and life as we
know it, we may need to learn a little about shepherding. A less familiar metaphor, perhaps, to most who read these lessons, the metaphor of
the good shepherd was familiar to the people in Jesus' day.

➤ Despite familiarity with sheep and shepherds, which were part and par-
cel of day-to-day life in first-century Palestine, the metaphor of the
good shepherd was not readily understood by the Jews. They wanted
Jesus to speak plainly instead of in "figures."

➤ No matter how Jesus tried to teach of God, resistance to his message
was strong.

1. How does the true shepherd enter the sheepfold as opposed to how thieves and robbers enter it?

2. What two things did Jesus call himself?

3. What does the hireling do?

4. What does the good shepherd do?

In John 10:1-18 Jesus used the pastoral imagery of the shepherd to continue his teaching. We assume the audience was still the group of Pharisees (9:40). The conversation took place sometime between the Feast of Tabernacles and the Feast of Dedication. The Feast of Tabernacles took place in the fall. The Feast of Dedication (Hanukkah) took place in the month of *Chislev* and falls close to Christmas.

## THE FEAST OF TABERNACLES (SUKKOTH)

One of the major festivals of the Jewish faith, the Festival of Tabernacles (also called "Booths" or "Ingathering"), is celebrated for eight days. In spirit very much like an American Thanksgiving, the feast originated as a fall thanksgiving holiday. The crops had been gathered. God had provided. Celebration could begin! Like holidays and holy days today, however, the Feast of Tabernacles was more than a simple celebration for abundant fields and vineyards. The feast also celebrated God's protection for the chosen people, symbolized best perhaps in the

Exodus experience. In that focal event for the Jewish people, the Jews were led forth from slavery in Egypt to the rigors of the desert. Without the security of permanent shelters, the Jews learned anew that God would shelter them and lead them in the days ahead.

The Feast of Tabernacles called upon the Jews to erect "booths"—roofless shelters of twigs, branches, and leaves— and to live within them throughout the course of the festival. Symbols of the harvest were brought within the booths, reminding dwellers that the God of the Exodus would continue to guide and shelter the people of Israel. Scriptures related to the Feast of Tabernacles include Exodus 23:16; 34:22; Leviticus 23:33-36; Numbers 28:26-31; Deuteronomy 16:13-17; and Ezekiel 45:25.

## Jesus the Good Shepherd

What is the context for Jesus speaking of sheep and shepherds? In chapter 9 a blind man who was healed became a follower of Jesus. Subsequently, the man was banned from the synagogue (9:34). This event may provide the context for a discussion of a "new fold," which an individual may enter.

Judea was mostly rocky ground more suited to raising sheep than farming. There was little grass, and the sheep often wandered off looking for a little patch. The shepherd was a stalwart and dedicated worker. The sheep were raised mainly for their wool rather than for meat; consequently the sheep often were in the care of their shepherd for quite some time. Not only would a shepherd know each one, the sheep would know the voice of the shepherd.

There were two kinds of sheepfolds in Palestine. There were sheepfolds in the villages where all the flocks were kept when they were brought down off the plateau at night. These had strong doors that were locked to protect the sheep, and the gatekeeper controlled who went in and out (3). The shepherd would check on his sheep by entering through the gate. The gatekeeper would recognize the shepherd and let him enter. A thief would climb over the wall to avoid the gatekeeper and steal a sheep. The sheep would hear the voice of their shepherd, be able to distinguish that voice from that of a stranger, and would willingly follow him. John 10:1-6 contrasted the true shepherd with deceitful pretenders.

## Jesus the Gate to the Sheepfold

The Jews knew about the relationship between sheep and shepherds, but they seemed to be having trouble understanding this figurative language. Jesus attempted to explain further with two applications of the analogy: the gate and the good shepherd.

In Jesus' day there was another type of sheepfold scattered on the hillsides where the sheep grazed. Many times the sheep were not brought into the village at night but were kept in these makeshift sheepfolds so that wild animals or thieves could not get at them. These sheepfolds were

walled-in areas without a roof or door (just an open space). The shepherd would lie down in front of the opening to protect the sheep. The shepherd himself was literally the gate.

Figuratively speaking, Jesus described himself as the gate (7), opening the way to God. To enter the sheepfold, a place of safety and security, one would have to go through the gate.

## Jesus the Responsible Shepherd

In Greek there are two words for *good*. *Agathos* refers to moral goodness. *Kalos* is good in the descriptive sense of lovely, beautiful, "a good thing." When Jesus is described as the good shepherd the word used is *kalos*. Jesus was more than a moral human being, but a good and pleasing Son, an entryway to God.

According to John, those who came before Jesus were thieves and robbers. He did not appear to be referring to the prophets and leaders of Israel; he had great respect for Moses and others. He may have been speaking of the Pharisees, the corrupt priests, or the Sadducees who controlled the Temple. Elsewhere Jesus called them a "den of robbers" (Mark 11:17). They may also refer to political rebels, zealots and insurrectionists who were numerous at that time, or any of the other opportunists of the day. Jesus may have been referring to the political leaders who sought gain by rubbing elbows with the Roman rulers. They came to destroy, but Jesus came to give life abundantly (10). Nor was Jesus like the hireling who was only out for personal gain and cared nothing for the sheep. The hireling's only concern was to produce bigger and better sheep and to save his own skin. The true shepherd was trained from a young age to be responsible for his sheep. If anything happened to a sheep, the shepherd had to prove to the other that it was not his fault. Amos 3:12, for example, talked about a shepherd retrieving two legs or a piece of an ear out of a lion's mouth. Exodus 22:13 stated the law: "If it was mangled by beasts, let it be brought as evidence; restitution shall not be made for the mangled remains."

## Jesus the Obedient Shepherd

The two short verses of 17 and 18 tell us much about Jesus. They tell us how his whole life was devoted to God. He was totally obedient to God. Like the shepherd who was totally responsible for his sheep, he *chose* to lay his life down for them. Even though God raised Jesus from the dead, *Jesus laid down his life.* He who was one with the will of God knew that God would not abandon him. He was not caught up in circumstances. He was in control of his own destiny. Jesus, the Good Shepherd, laid down his life for his flock, not because he was forced to; he willingly did so (15:13).

## THE FEAST OF DEDICATION

Known in modern times primarily as *Hanukkah*, the Feast of Dedication is a Jewish festival celebrating the purification of the Temple during the Maccabean revolt. It recalls a time of religious persecution, in 165 B.C., when the Temple altar was polluted by pagan sacrifice. Eventually, the siege of Jerusalem was broken. The Temple was ritually cleansed and a new sacrificial altar built. First Maccabees 4:50-51 tells the story. Three years from the time when the altar had been polluted, the new altar was dedicated (1 Maccabees 4:52-58) amidst great celebration.

In time, the Feast of Dedication (perhaps because of its calendar proximity to the Feast of Tabernacles) became like a second Feast of Tabernacles, similar to the way in which Christmas and New Year's Day "blend" together for much of the secular world. Again, 2 Maccabees tells the story "They celebrated it for eight days with rejoicing in the manner of the festival of booths, remembering how not long before, during the festival of booths, they had been wandering in the mountains and caves like wild animals" (10:6).

As the Feast of Tabernacles was symbolized in the building of booths, the Feast of Dedication was symbolized by light. Why? A legend tells that a small amount of holy oil was discovered in the Temple during the time of purification. Poured into the Temple lamp, it was enough to light the lamp for eight days until additional oil could be obtained. Today, Jews continue to celebrate Hanukkah, in part by lighting a home candelabra called a *menorah*.

John 10:19-42 debates whether Jesus was demon possessed or Son of God. At the Feast of Dedication Jesus stated again his claim of his relation to God and the promise of eternal life. His identity was questioned. Is he the Christ, the Anointed One? The Jews challenged Jesus to make a statement about himself. (He had not directly claimed to be the Messiah in public, only privately to the Samaritan woman in 4:26 and the blind man in 9:37.) Perhaps Jesus knew he would be mistaken, that his questioners were not sincere, or that further claims would only get him into more trouble. Or, perhaps his hour had not yet come.

## Jesus Is Rejected

John 10:22-42 tells of the last controversy between Jesus and the religious authorities, which paved the way for his betrayal and death. During the Feast of Dedication, while Jesus was in the Temple, Jesus spoke of his close relationship with God. While not openly stating he was the Messiah, Jesus spoke of that relationship in the most intimate and challenging of terms:"The works I do in my Father's name testify to me; but you do not believe, because you do not belong to my sheep. My sheep hear my voice. I know them, and they follow me. I give them eternal life, and they will never again perish" (25-27). Angered, the Jews attempted to stone Jesus; stoning was the penalty for blasphemy.

Escaping an attempt to arrest him, Jesus went across the Jordon River to Perea where John the Baptist had baptized. Many seekers followed him there, according to these final verses of chapter 10, and many came to believe in him.

## Dimension 3:
## What Does the Bible Mean to Us?

## An Image Immortalized in Our Hearts

The image of the good shepherd is one of the best known, most beloved "word pictures" of the Bible. Numerous paintings, sculptures, and stained glass depict the shepherd. Possibly every child who has attended Sunday school has learned about Jesus, the Good Shepherd. It is an image immortalized in our hearts.

Lambs are a symbol of innocence and complete vulnerability. All of us, at one time or another in our lives, feel vulnerable. We need protection. We need to feel safe in the arms of the Shepherd. And we, like sheep, are quick to stray. We need a shepherd. Jesus loves and cares for us as a shepherd loves and cares for a flock.

Quite another angle on John 10:1-18 is the dispute over leadership. The use of the shepherd analogy illustrates Jesus as leader, guide, and founder of the church. True, Jesus is concerned with our individual well being, but we should not overlook the sense of the shepherd as leader of the flock.

There were false leaders, "thieves and bandits," imposters, charlatans during this time, continuing even to this day. There were those who attempted to steal the sheep, those who tried to steal them away from Christ. And there was, out on the rocky hillsides, always the threat of wolves waiting for an opportune moment to attack and destroy. There was the hireling who simply took the job of shepherding for money, who would run at the sign of danger. Jesus gave strong warning against all of these individuals.

Of course these threats are still with us. It is not difficult to draw a comparison with those who live contrary to the gospel, those who say they care but really have ulterior motives, those who use the church for personal gain. It is difficult to say which is worse: the wolf that devours the lamb or the hireling who stands by and lets it happen.

It may not, however, serve us well to be too quick to point a finger at others and call them thieves and robbers in a judgmental way. We can be aware, however, that thieves and robbers do exist among us. Lest we become thieves and robbers ourselves, we must daily strive to follow Jesus.

## Jesus Offers Pasture

We have heard that Jesus supplies the bread of life, the living water, and light to the world. In this passage we learn that he offers pasture, security, and guidance, a place of safety, a home. We need spiritual leaders to guide us today. Humans, unlike sheep, have a strong will and intellect that cause us to go our own way. Even more than sheep, we stray and resist the guiding hand of leadership. Human beings pursue all kinds of tangents. We need strong leaders to bring us together in a unity of purpose and vision. The word *pastor* comes from the Latin word for shepherd. Today we especially need shepherds with Christlike qualities to lead the church.

Jesus is the entry for believers seeking a relationship with God. He is the gate. The gate leads to both promise and challenge. The entrance promises something new inside, but it is a challenge in that a gate can be both welcoming and inviting, or it can seem forbidding and a barrier. Who is able to enter? Jesus said it was those sheep whom God had given. For some this sounds exclusive: some are in, others are not. God, however, is no one's exclusive property. There has been some question over the meaning of 10:16. Does it mean there is one true fold, one true church, and no salvation outside it? Or does it mean that there is one flock that brings together many faiths and cultures? The unity of the flock does not come out of being forced or funneled into one true church. The unity does not mean there is only one idea of God, only one way of worshiping God, one true form of church government. It does mean that our common bond is Jesus Christ. In the world there is much division between beliefs, nations, and cultures. The universality of Christ crosses these boundaries.

The unity always presents a paradox. Jesus is the gate; some come inside, others remain outside. The Christian's task may well be to live and share with those outside in love and acceptance, inviting others in, rather than declaring them outside the fold. We are called to a unique and critical ministry with the unchurched in these times.

## Accept Him on Faith

In John 16:25 Jesus spoke of a future time when he would no longer speak in figures but would openly declare the truth about God. This was in response to the Jews who wanted him to speak plainly. The impatience of the Jews is familiar, for we too would like to have it all spelled out for us in plain talk. But it is not that simple. Jesus' teachings were not simple and shallow; understanding them requires trust as well as reason. Jesus explained his mission, but they did not believe.

There comes a point at which self-justification is no longer useful. Jesus justified himself, stating his authority. At some point rationalizations had done all they could do.

One has to accept Jesus on faith, John tells us. Jesus' actions, his works, and his integrity speak more about who he is than anything he could say. Unbelief does not necessarily come from inadequate evidence. The failure to understand may not be so much an intellectual problem, but an unwillingness to try to believe, an unwillingness to step through the gate.

## Dimension 4:
## A Daily Bible Journey Plan

*Day 1:* **John 10:1-6**

*Day 2:* **John 10:7-18**

*Day 3:* **John 10:19-20**

*Day 4:* **John 10:21-24**

*Day 5:* **John 10:25-30**

*Day 6:* **John 10:31-39**

*Day 7:* **John 10:40-42**

**John 11:1-57**

**7**

# *T*HE RAISING OF LAZARUS

## *What to Watch For*

John 11 tells the story of the raising of Lazarus, the climax of all the signs in this Gospel. Here begins the culmination of Jesus' life in his death and resurrection. In some ways the entire Gospel hinges upon this story. As you read, watch for the following emphases:

➤ Lazarus and his sisters Martha and Mary were friends of Jesus from Bethany. The sisters sent word to Jesus that Lazarus was ill. Jesus did not come at once, but waited two days.
➤ When Jesus did arrive in Bethany, Lazarus was already dead and the house was filled with mourners. Martha and Mary did not understand why Jesus had not come to help their brother at once for they knew he had the power to heal.
➤ Jesus knew the raising of Lazarus was an opportunity to show God's glory and the glory of the Son. He called Lazarus forth from the tomb.
➤ The raising of Lazarus is what prompted the authorities to plan to put Jesus to death. It is no coincidence that the one called "the resurrection and the life" would choose to give life to another, knowing that he, himself, would meet soon with the cross.

In previous sessions we have learned that Jesus spoke of himself as the Good Shepherd who would lay down his life for the sheep (10:11-18). In this session, we will learn that Jesus will risk his life to renew the life of his friend Lazarus. The raising of Lazarus sets the stage for the Passion event.

1. How did Jesus respond when he learned of Lazarus' illness?

2. What was the gist of the conversation between Jesus and the disciples concerning going to Judea to be with the family?

3. What did Jesus and his disciples find when they arrived in Bethany?

4. What did Jesus tell Martha and what did he do, according to John?

5. What happened as a result of the raising of Lazarus?

## Dimension 2:
## What Does the Bible Mean?

### Setting the Stage for a Sign

Martha, Mary, and Lazarus were friends of Jesus. Their home was in Bethany east of Jerusalem (11:18). It was a kind of haven or resting place for Jesus. John identified Mary as the one who anointed Jesus (11:2), an event described in the next chapter.

When Lazarus became ill, Martha and Mary notified Jesus (3). The message to Jesus was simply stated, "Lord, he whom you love is ill." Obviously, there was great friendship among these four. There simply was no question that Jesus would not quickly come to the aid of this family!

### The Drama Intensifies

Having learned of his friend's illness, Jesus did not immediately travel to Bethany. Instead, he acknowledged that Lazarus' illness was an opportunity to show the glory of God and for the Son to be glorified. Two days passed! Jesus seemed almost willing for his friend to die! Acting in his own time, after two days had passed, Jesus discussed the trip to Bethany with his disciples.

The disciples hesitated because the Judeans had tried to stone Jesus (8). They were not stupid! Returning to Judea was akin to placing one's hand in the lion's mouth, knowing that the lion was hungry! Furthermore, returning to Judea may have been more like placing the hands of Jesus and the Twelve in the lion's mouth. Is it any wonder that the disciples cautioned Jesus against the trip?

At first glance, Jesus' answer in verses 9-10 seemed strange: "Are there not twelve hours of daylight? Those who walk during the day do not stumble, because they see the light of this world. But those who walk at night stumble, because the light is not in them." Once again, Jesus was attempting to put his disciples' fears at rest by reminding them that "his hour has not yet come" (7:30). He could travel safely to Bethany.

It may be helpful to remember that any illness was of grave concern during this era of primitive medical care. However, in this case, it was not only the lack of medical care that was significant in the story but the sister's belief that Jesus could heal Lazarus. Unlike others who sought Jesus in times of medical crises, Mary and Martha did not ask Jesus to come. They took it for granted that, once notified, Jesus would come.

## The Hour Had Not Yet Come

We know from earlier passages in John that Jesus would not be hurried. It was clear that Jesus would act according to the will of God and not according to what people wanted him to do. We saw this in the wedding at Cana, in his words to the crowd who wanted him to produce bread, and to his brothers about going to the feast. Jesus' life would be as God planned. He would not act or refuse to act out of fear. The time allowed for his ministry was limited and each aspect needed to be carried out at the appointed hour no matter the danger or inconvenience.

Frequently, John used the words of Jesus to reflect a double meaning. Verses 9 and 10 exemplify this well. On one level Jesus may have been talking about making the trip during the day before nightfall so that he and the Twelve could see. On another level, of course, Jesus has told us he is the light of the world. Without Christ there is darkness and we stumble. On yet another level Jesus was reminding his disciples that there was little concern about traveling to Judea. To wait to go at night, to sneak around to avoid confrontation, was not what was called for at this time.

## Remarkable Courage

Jesus made another strange remark. He told the disciples that Lazarus was asleep (11). Sleep was a common euphemism for death in the Bible (see Matthew 9:24; 1 Thessalonians 4:13; 1 Corinthians 15:6), but the disciples did not get it. They thought Lazarus must be better and resting well—and therefore, there was no need for a risk-filled trip to Judea. So Jesus spoke more plainly and told them Lazarus was dead. Further, he said Lazarus' death would prove to be a blessing to the disciples in that their own faith would be increased as a result.

William Barclay, legendary for his insights into the disciples, indicates that at least one disciple was attuned to the reality of the situation. "At that moment it might well have been that the disciples might have refused to follow Jesus; but then one lonely voice spoke up. They were all feeling that to go to Jerusalem was to go to die, and they were hanging back, for no [man] likes to undertake a course which is suicide. . . . Thomas displayed the highest kind of courage" (The Daily Study Bible Series, *The Gospel of John*, Volume 2, Westminster Press, 1956; page 101). Thomas' words were simple and grim, "Let us also go, that we may die with him" (16).

## A House of Mourning

When they arrived, Lazarus had been dead four days. The four days may have been important as a way of making the point that Lazarus was truly dead and not in a coma. Also it was popular Jewish belief that body and soul were separated after one had been dead for three days. Then and only then was one considered truly dead with no chance of resuscitation.

Burial in Palestine occurred as soon after death as possible because of the climate. Fine ointments were used to anoint the body, which was then wrapped in cloth. Because a Jewish funeral was attended by many persons, Jesus found a crowd at the house of Martha and Mary. In verse 20 Martha met Jesus—an unusual thing for a mourner to do. At this time, mourners traditionally stayed at home during the first week, except for visits to the tomb. Mary stayed at home—Martha veared from tradition.

Knowing the power of Jesus, Martha said to him, "Lord, if you had been here, my brother would not have died" (21). She wondered why Jesus had not come immediately when he received word. Then she spoke in faith that she knew God would grant Jesus whatever he asked (22). Jesus told her that her brother would rise again (23). Martha thought Jesus was saying that Lazarus would be resurrected on the last day, a common belief among some Jews (see Mark 12:18-27; Acts 23:6-8; 24:15, 21). There was no notion of life after death in the Old Testament. The Hebrews believed all human souls went to Sheol, which was not Hell, but the abode of the dead. Then Jesus said to Martha, "I am the resurrection and the life." This important verse (25) says that resurrection is not just something that is to come at the last day, but something Jesus gives now, a present reality.

## "Do You Believe This?"

Jesus said that those who believe in him shall never die. Physical death is not the end. Through Jesus Christ we are headed for the life to come with God.

Jesus asked Martha if she believed, and she replied that she did. She went to get Mary at the house, and Mary left quickly to see Jesus followed by the mourners (29-31). She too chided Jesus for not arriving sooner. Jesus saw Mary and all the people weeping. Open display of sorrow was common and considered a way of honoring the deceased. Jesus was deeply distressed. Like all humans he experienced pain and sorrow.

## Jesus Raises Lazarus

Jesus asked where the body had been laid, and they took him there (34). A Palestinian tomb was usually a natural cave or carved from rock with a large stone rolled in front of the entrance. Jesus asked that the stone be rolled away. (The similarities with his own tomb are striking.) Martha thought perhaps Jesus wished to look once more upon the face of his friend, but she reminded Jesus that Lazarus had been dead four days, and his body would already be decaying. Persisting, Jesus reminded her that she would witness the glory of God (40). After prayer Jesus called Lazarus out of the tomb. Lazarus walked out wrapped in burial cloth and bandages. Jesus did not raise Lazarus for his own prestige, but so that those present could know the power of God.

Only John recorded the raising of Lazarus. The other three Gospels contain accounts of others being raised: Jairus' daughter (Matthew 9:18-26; Mark 5:21-43; Luke 8:40-56) and the widow's son (Luke 7:11-16). In these cases the raising was immediately after death.

One may wonder, if the story of Lazarus is authentic, why do the other three Gospels omit it? Though the Synoptics do not recount it, the story sounds like material found in Luke. Luke recorded the story of a man named Lazarus and a rich man in 16:19-31. This story also deals with death and resurrection. The story John told may stem from an early tradition about Jesus.

## The Pharisees Plot to Kill Jesus

Lazarus and Jesus—one life regained, another's death forged. As seen in verses 45-53, the decision to put Jesus to death is culminated in the giving of life to Lazarus. Could Jesus have known this?

The Sanhedrin, the ruling council for the Jewish community, was made up of Pharisees and Sadducees. The Pharisees were not a political party, but were concerned with obedience to the law. The Sadducees were a political party, mostly made up of wealthy aristocrats. The priests were Sadducees in power at the time, willing to collaborate with the Romans. They reasoned and plotted that if Jesus gained a large following, he could displace them and cause civil disorder. They were only in power at the whim of the Romans and could easily lose their power and position of privilege. Caiaphas, the high priest, spoke. It was a Jewish belief that the high priest spoke for God; he was the channel of God's word. In this case, Caiaphas said it was better for one man to die than to risk having a nation destroyed. Little did he know the truth of his words. Jesus did die for the nation and for all others.

## The End of Public Ministry

Throughout John's Gospel there is the foreshadowing of Jesus' death, but we are told his "hour is not yet come." This chapter ends Jesus' public ministry and begins the intensification of the coming of that hour. Jesus could no longer go about openly. In verse 54 Jesus went to the village of Ephraim (fifteen miles north of Jerusalem). In Jerusalem people were preparing for the Passover feast. There were several days of purifications and cleansing required. Those Jews of the Dispersion who lived among Gentiles had to purify themselves for the feast. They began looking for Jesus. They wondered if he would dare come to the feast since he was wanted by the authorities.

## Dimension 3:
## What Does the Bible Mean to Us?

### A Promise of Eternal Life

John tells a moving account of the raising of Lazarus, a story which is not just about a tragedy, not just about a death of a friend, but a miracle for a family at Bethany. The miracle of the raising of Lazarus had a symbolic importance. It showed the tragic nature of humanity, sick unto death as we are, and the miracle of life in Christ who calls us forth into life. Jesus loved Lazarus, as he loves all of us. Jesus gave him life as he does all of us. The story is not so much about how a man came back to life; the details are sketchy. Only two verses describe the actual miracle. It is a story about the life that Jesus gives through his death and resurrection.

It was not just compassion for friends that moved Jesus to bring Lazarus back to life, but rather the opportunity for Jesus to demonstrate the glory of God. In this sign, in particular, Jesus would be glorified as the Son of God.

The story is powerful not just because it is about some amazing feat, nor because it stresses physical life. It is perhaps most meaningful to us because it holds the promise for spiritual and eternal life through Christ. The renewing of physical life was but a sign of eternal life in Jesus Christ.

Why was Jesus moved to demonstrate his love for humankind, knowing that the miracle at Bethany could only rekindle the authorities' rejection of him? Why risk losing one's own life to save the life of another?

While Jesus was compassionate toward human beings, his purpose was not simply to answer the physical needs of humans. He came to show us God. Tragic things happen in life, and we may wonder why God allows it. God, as revealed in Jesus, does not cause suffering in this way. God cries with us in our pain just as Jesus wept over Lazarus with Mary and Martha. In these painful times, there is an opportunity for us to enter into a closer relationship with God.

# Jesus Is the Resurrection and the Life

Martha was a follower of Jesus. She believed in his power. She also believed, as did others of her day, in a future resurrection. Her understanding, like our own, was limited. Jesus, however, gave new meaning to the resurrection. He not only brings resurrection and life; he *is* the Resurrection and the Life. When we believe in Jesus, we are resurrected and have life now. We rise above the death of sin—the bitterness, the fear, the frustration—all the forces that work against life and are so much a part of a life that is lived apart from God. When we believe in Jesus Christ, our physical deaths become our pathway to eternal life with God.

Do we stop and think about how Jesus Christ is life for us? Many people read this to mean that Jesus offers some kind of life after death. While Jesus does offer eternal life, in saying "I am the resurrection and the life," Jesus was also saying "I am the difference between death and life. I am the point at which death leaves off and life begins. I make the promise of eternal life begin now." The Resurrection is a present reality in the life of believers and not just something that is to come. Do we pin all our hopes on the future, overlooking the presence and power of Christ in our lives in the present? Do we wish for what could be or what might have been instead of acting in the present on the life that Christ gives us? Can we do something, do we need to do something now, that reflects the life we have through Jesus Christ?

## How Does God Intervene?

At funerals it is often customary to try to comfort the bereaved by extolling the qualities of heaven. While this is a valid comfort for some, sometimes it does not comfort but only heightens the pain of loss. The grieving ask, "Why did God not intervene in life to prevent my husband, daughter, son, mother, or father from dying? Why does God not act?" This passage in John tells us that action is exactly what God does do. God acted and acts in Jesus Christ to give life to the dying, which includes all of us.

Jesus, in showing us something about God, gives us life. He also teaches us something about prayer in this passage. He prays here not a prayer just for the benefit of the onlookers; he is not going to God to help him out of a troubled spot. Jesus was not asking for power, but thanking God for the power that God had already given him. Jesus showed us that we too can have this kind of power, this kind of relationship with God.

The text indicates that seeing Jesus' power to bring life would confirm the faith of his followers. Willing, expectant believers may see God's power and glory. There must be a willingness to believe. The miracle is a sign to those of faith to whom Jesus gives life. Some, even though they witnessed it, did not believe. The final line of the story of the rich man and Lazarus in Luke is that even if someone did rise from the dead, there would be those who would not believe it. Do we have that willingness to trust? Do we look to Jesus to relieve all our needs and wants or can we move beyond that to a deeper level of faith and find in him new life? Do we believe in Jesus because he was a worker of signs, because he could give physical life? Even some who witnessed the miracle failed to believe the signs, which according to John got Jesus into trouble.

The Synoptic Gospels infer that the reasons for Jesus' death were some of the things he said and did that were critical of the status quo, such as the cleansing of the Temple. John's Gospel conveys that idea. Although some praised Jesus for his miracles and works, the raising of Lazarus was the critical thing that led to his condemnation. John saw this miracle as the last straw, the definitive cause of Jesus' arrest and death. Even though he could do the works of God and some believed, it provoked anger and fear enough to get him arrested and killed. For John the giving of life led to Jesus' own death. It is through his death and resurrection, through the cross, that Jesus is glorified and becomes the Resurrection and the Life for us.

Sometimes we do not fully appreciate the impact of the statement, "I am the resurrection and the life." Quite simply, it means everything! It means the difference between life and death for the believer. Whoever lives and believes in him shall never die.

## Dimension 4:
## A Daily Bible Journey Plan

*Day 1:* **John 11:1-6**

*Day 2:* **John 11:7-16**

*Day 3:* **John 11:17-27**

*Day 4:* **John 11:28-37**

*Day 5:* **John 11:38-44**

*Day 6:* **John 11:45-53**

*Day 7:* **John 11:54-57**

# 8

# THE ENTRY INTO JERUSALEM

## *What to Watch For*

Jesus' entry into Jerusalem initiated the final week of Jesus' life. As you read this familiar story, watch for the following emphases:

➤ John described how the enthusiastic crowds followed Jesus or came to meet Jesus because he had raised Lazarus. They waved palms and shouted "hosanna."

➤ Jesus came riding in on a donkey's colt. The crowds praised him as a conqueror, but Jesus was not the conqueror of a nation; his victory was through the cross.

➤ On this occasion some Greeks wanted to approach Jesus. Several important teachings followed this exchange. One was that through his death, many more could have life. Something must die in order to give life.

➤ John recorded that Jesus would die to draw all people unto himself and cast out Satan. Many did not understand; their eyes were blinded and hearts were hardened. But Jesus was the light and any who believed would not remain in darkness.

1. Describe the actions of the crowds in 12:12-19.

2. What was the Pharisees' reaction to Jesus' arrival in Jerusalem?

3. Describe the actions of the Greeks (Gentiles) and Jesus' response.

4. What are some of Jesus' teachings in verses 27-50?

### Jesus—the Hope of the Crowds

Jerusalem was crowded for the Passover season. Some have speculated on
the number that would have been present. Some Bible scholars believe
that as many as one hundred thousand persons might come to Jerusalem
for the Passover. Rumors circulated that Jesus, the one who brought
Lazarus back from the dead, was coming to Jerusalem. There was a crowd
waiting for him; another group had accompanied him from Bethany. Six
days before the Passover feast, Jesus rode in on a young donkey. The
crowds waved palm branches as if they were greeting a victorious conqueror or hero of battle. For John, the enthusiasm of the crowd was due to
the Lazarus miracle. John tells us this several times (9, 17). Chapter 11
announces that the purpose of the raising of Lazarus was so that the Son of
God might be glorified. John 12:23 announces that the hour of that glorification has come.

The sight and sounds of the crowds, swelling by the minute, caused
panic among the Jewish authorities. It seemed that many people were turning to Jesus. According to the text, the people shouted,

"Hosanna!
Blessed is the one who comes in the name of
  the Lord—
  the King of Israel!" (13)

This cry of the crowd is a quotation from Psalm 118:25-26, a psalm used during major Jewish festivals. Psalm 118 was part of the Passover ritual; it is a psalm of thanksgiving for deliverance in battle. The crowd saw in Jesus one who would lead the victory against Roman oppression and lead the Jews to a position of prominence. He was their hope and salvation.

## Jesus Came in Peace

By riding the donkey Jesus was deliberately claiming to be the Messiah, enacting the words of Zechariah 9:9. John recalled some of these words in verse 15. When one rode on a horse, it was symbolic of going to war, but the donkey signified that Jesus came in peace. The crowd misunderstood the sign of Lazarus and tried to make Jesus king. Recall John 6:15 when the crowds tried to make Jesus king because of the sign of feeding the multitude. A king would have ridden on a horse or used a chariot. As in Zechariah, Jesus came humbly, riding on an ass. Even though the authorities were threatening to kill him, Jesus rode into Jerusalem in the middle of a mob. He did not run off, but came openly, taking the opportunity to show who he was and what he was about even on his way to the end. To the Pharisees it seemed that "the world has gone after him!" (19) It was an exaggeration, but truer than they knew.

In chapter 12 John describes three scenes. The first is the anointing by Mary at Bethany. The second is the entry into Jerusalem. The third scene describes the Greeks' request to see Jesus and Jesus' subsequent teachings. The anointing story was also relayed in Mark and Matthew. This session focuses on the second and third scenes, which take place during Passover week.

In John 12:20 some Greeks went to the disciple named Philip and asked to see Jesus. They may have approached Philip because his name was Greek. They may have felt he might be sympathetic to them. Philip told Andrew. Together they told Jesus of the request. Jesus responded in a puzzling way about how a grain of wheat falls to the ground and spreads its fruit. The wheat drops its seeds which then, in turn, grow and do the same (24). It is assumed that Jesus approved of the Greeks coming to him, although we are not told that the Greeks actually came before Jesus at this point. Why did Jesus answer the request as he did? He spoke of sacrifice, of dying in order to give life. Jesus was saying that by his death, he would be available to all. When "his hour" came he would draw all unto him. The glorified Christ would be present to all people in all times. This was especially important to John's listener's because they were distanced in time from the events.

The phrase "Very truly I tell you" or "Truly, truly I say unto you," so characteristic in the Gospel of John, is a double amen sometimes translated as "I solemnly assure you." It occurs about twenty-five times in John, as in 1:51; 3:3; 3:11; 5:19; 6:47; 8:51.

The next few verses contain a handful of teachings of Jesus. "The hour has come for the Son of Man to be glorified" (23). Things had been building up, tension was mounting. Jesus knew it was time for him, the one who had come with a message, to take that message to the limit, the limit of the cross.

When some heard Jesus say that the Son of Man would be glorified, they thought he meant that he would be empowered, enthroned. (See the glossary for the meaning of the term *Son of Man*, page 112.) Jesus meant that the glorification would come through his death. He talked about how a grain of wheat has to die in order to start a new growth. It breaks off and falls to the ground leaving its seed. That particular grain dies in order to give life to a new seed.

Why should one get so involved in this world, this life, only to lose it? One who realizes this life is fleeting and stakes claim to life in Christ truly lives. To love life and go after it with a vengeance is only to lose life. To give up and renounce the ways of the world is to find life.

## Jesus Was Troubled

In verse 27 Jesus spoke of his troubled soul. He was afraid, but he did not ask God to save him from the cross. Jesus continued his obedience to God. He knew that God would be glorified and he spoke this in prayer. According to the text there was an answer, a voice from heaven that confirmed Jesus' words. It was spoken for the sake of the people, but they did not understand it. They thought it was thunder or an angel, but certainly not God. The Jews at one time believed that God spoke directly. They knew that God's voice was audible to Samuel (1 Samuel 3:1-4) and Elijah

(1 Kings 19:1-18), among others. The voice of God is described in Psalm 29 as a thundering voice, a powerful voice, but also a voice that brings peace. During the time of Jesus, however, God was understood to be far off and less directly communicative.

> To follow the light makes us Jesus' children—children that follow as in play.

God spoke through the high priest (recall Caiaphas). Jesus heard the voice of God directly. This occurence was yet another event that amazed and confounded the Jewish onlookers.

Jesus told them that when he would be lifted up, the ruler of the world would be cast out. Clearly, Jesus was referring to Satan in verse 31—the "ruler of this world." (See 14:30, 16:11.) Jesus' going to the cross would break the power of evil in the world. In being crucified, Jesus would draw all of humanity to him. All people in every place and time would be affected by Jesus' death on the cross. The crowd responded in verse 34 that they had heard that the Messiah was to endure forever, not die. The Son of Man was supposed to rule over an everlasting kingdom. Psalm 89:36 cries, "His line shall continue forever." Jesus shared that the light would be among them for a little while. He advised followers to learn to walk in the light while there was still time. "Believe in the light," he told them, "so that you may become children of the light."

## They Did Not Believe

Jesus then departed from the people, and John reported that even though Jesus had done great things, many did not believe. He quoted Isaiah saying that the prophet's words had come to pass. The first passage was from Isaiah 53:1-2. The prophet asked if there was anyone who believed him and anyone who would recognize that his words came from God. The second passage was derived from Isaiah 6:9-10. This passage about the call of Isaiah is quoted several times in the New Testament (see Matthew 13:14-15; Luke 8:10; Acts 28; Romans 11:8). The intent of the passage implies that God causes people not to hear, not to believe. Isaiah, however, was discouraged about those who refused to believe. It seemed to him that God had caused people to turn away from him. In the mind of the Jews, God caused everything. They believed that everything occurred according to God's plan and purposes. There would always be those who refused to believe, but God could use that unbelief to further his purpose.

Even the authorities and rulers who did believe in Jesus were afraid to say so publicly. They were more concerned with pleasing their peers than with pleasing God. Verses 44-50 summarize Jesus' teachings. John wrote that Jesus cried out, but previously in verse 36 he had left the Jews. It has been suggested that verses 44-50 should follow 36a before Jesus leaves. Perhaps the passage was rearranged by a later editor. John did not say where Jesus was when he said these words, nor to whom he spoke. These words were Jesus' last public teaching according to John. He says that to believe in him is to believe in the one who sent him. In Jesus, God and humanity meet. John stressed two things which he had said before: Jesus did not come to the world to condemn but to save. Yet Jesus' coming into the world involves judgment. Not to believe is to judge oneself. Jesus concluded his teaching by saying once again that his authority was not from himself but from God (Deuteronomy 18:18). What was that commandment? It was, according to verse 50, eternal life.

## Dimension 3:
## What Does the Bible Mean to Us?

### No Cross, No Crown

The triumphant entry of Jesus has been made known to us through the telling of the story, through art, and through our worship experience. On Palm Sunday we recall in our worship both the joyous adoration of Jesus and the sorrow of his coming death. On Palm Sunday our sense of being part of the crowd, part of the processional, may come home to us. Every Sunday, really, worshipers come from their various, diverse lives and go into worship in unity.

"No cross, no crown. No pain, no gain."

Some of us come because we are curious. Some of us come because our neighbors do. Some of us come because we heard or think Jesus can do something for us. Some of us come because we believe and seek to know the God that Jesus shares with us. We come with varying expectations. We come praising and asking him to save us. Sometimes we do not understand or are unclear about our expectations. Are we looking for a deliverer? Like the Greeks, we may wonder if we dare approach him.

Jesus' kind of leadership was not the kind that was expected. His success was not by ordinary human standards. He was not the king that would win the victory for the nation. He was the king that would go to the cross for them and us. His dying made life available for all of us. There are no restrictions on who can approach Jesus. He died for every nation, race, and people.

Something must die in order to give life. That is the cycle of life and death as we know it in nature. To extend the analogy for Jesus, "no cross, no crown." For us it is the same. "No pain, no gain." Life is a series of ups and downs, gains and losses. Something has to be given up, must fade or die, for something else to come into full bloom. Sometimes we have to make sacrifices for a greater good to come about in our lives. We may have to give up our personal goals, wants, or desires in order to serve God. Life lived only for oneself is barren and empty. It is only in service to others that we truly have life and bear fruit.

The message to us is also that getting caught up in the worries or even the triumphs of life is futile. We sometimes act as if life itself hinged on every phone call, every task ahead that must be done. Success or failure in this life is fleeting, so why be caught up in it? It is only when we give up or hand over our futile attempts to control everything that we really have life. To follow Jesus is to "let go" of the world, to release our dependance on things, possessions, worries, accomplishments.

## A Victory Won

These final days of Jesus' life as told by John can bolster Christian faith. Jesus did not turn back. We can understand, even feel, his anguish. For all our sakes he went forward to glorify God's name. John wrote about a voice from heaven that thundered from the sky. That same voice sounds down through the centuries saying, "thy name be glorified." The saving, redeeming power of God will come forth and go into action. If we listen, we can hear that voice. Jesus went forward to be lifted up and, in doing so, dethroned the ruler of the world once and for all. While many would argue that Satan is still in power, Satan's power is no longer the final word. For each and every follower of Christ, there is a victory already won, but also a victory still to be won. Every Christian has to work out that victory in his or her own faith journey. Each time our faith falters or we find ourselves turning away from God or losing sight of the mark, we open the door for the ruler of the world to gain a foothold. Weekly, daily, hourly we re-tune our instruments, correct our vision, navigate our path, in the knowledge of what Christ has made possible for us.

God works in our lives. Yet that knowledge has the effect sometimes of making us shut our eyes and ears to God. We close ourselves off from God. We cannot imagine that God would love us or want us, so we resist. Accepting the fact that we need God and that God loves and needs us is difficult. God knows that people will be hostile and rebellious; that reality is nothing new to God. Jesus spoke and lived the truth. The truth is sometimes not what people want to hear. The truth is bound to blind eyes and harden hearts. Through faith our eyes are opened and our hearts made soft.

## Afraid to Go Public?

Some of the Pharisees did believe in Jesus, but they were afraid to go public. They were ashamed and afraid of what people might think. They put others over God. John unequivocally condemned their half-way faith.

Christians today suffer from the same malady. We believe in Jesus, but some of us may be afraid to tell others. We are concerned with what others might think. We want to fit in. We want to be liked. We do not want to be seen as fanatical or different.

Christians are called to be different. We do not need to make a big show of our faith. Christ does not need or want an ostentatious display from us. We can live our life in faith; and if we do, our belief in Jesus Christ will be reflected in the way we think, in our actions, and in our statements. We do not need to be concerned for what others may think of us. We do need to be concerned about living as God would want us to live.

Most of us are accountable to others in some way, to the structures and institutions of human life. Ultimately, however, our accountability is to God. As Jesus rode into Jerusalem that final week, he displayed for all the world to see his accountability to God.

## Dimension 4:
## A Daily Bible Journey Plan

*Day 1:* **John 12:1-11**

*Day 2:* **John 12:12-15**

*Day 3:* **John 12:16-19**

*Day 4:* **John 12:20-26**

*Day 5:* **John 12:27-36a**

*Day 6:* **John 12:36b-43**

*Day 7:* **John 12:44-50**

# *T*HE LAST SUPPER

## *What to Watch For*

Chapter 13 describes the last meal before the Passover feast during which Jesus washed the feet of the disciples. Although it was an act that is not readily understood, John interpreted it for his readers. Watch for these emphases as you read:

➤ Jesus' act of cleansing makes it possible to symbolically enter into faith. In ancient Palestine one had to wash the dirt and dust from feet upon entering a house. Likewise, humans must be washed clean in order to enter into the house of faith.

➤ For a teacher to engage in such a task as washing feet reversed ordinary human expectations and demonstrated the kind of humble service and sacrificial love we are to show one another. Jesus served us; we are to serve others.

➤ At the meal, the betrayer of Jesus was revealed to be Judas. Again, those present did not readily understand.

➤ Jesus began his farewell to his disciples and gave his new commandment of love. The chapter closes with Jesus foretelling the denial of Peter three times "before the cock crows" (38).

1. What did Jesus do during the supper just before Passover, according to John?

2. What was Jesus' response when Peter objected to having his feet washed by Jesus?

3. What did Jesus tell the disciples after he had finished washing their feet?

4. After Judas had gone out, what did Jesus talk about?

### Jesus Washes the Disciples' Feet

There are twenty-one chapters in the Gospel of John. John has Jesus' public ministry close with chapter 12. Nine chapters—nearly half of the Gospel of John—remain; John's major focus clearly was the Passion story. Chapter 13 begins the material known as the "pre-Passion" narrative. The story of the footwashing is one of the most beautiful examples of love and humility in all of literature. It clearly shows the character of Jesus as loving servant. Jesus was aware that the hour of his glorification was near. He knew the fate of the world depended upon him. Even possessing the glory of God, he took on the humble task of washing feet.

John 13:1 indicates that this took place "before the festival of the Passover." For John this last supper was not the Passover meal, as it was in the other Gospels. John dated the final meal *on the day before* the eve of Passover. Jesus died on Friday, the eve of Passover. This was the day that the lambs were slain in preparation for the Passover meal. Coincidence? Probably not. John may have intended to say that Jesus himself is the true paschal lamb. Verse 13:1 is an introduction to the "book of passion" or the "book of glory," which brings up the love of Jesus. Jesus has loved his own "to the end." He loved them both to the end of his life and to the very limits of the possible. John demonstrated the nature of that love with the footwashing story.

In verse 3 John expressed God's ultimate sovereignty and authority. Jesus knew that, while he was on earth, all God's authority was given to him. God entrusted Jesus to carry out God's purpose. Jesus knew he had come from God and would return.

Jesus might have considered himself above such a lowly task as washing feet or might not have wanted to waste his limited time tending to such matters. Instead he acted to serve his disciples, to do what must be done. Jesus also was aware, we are told, that one of the disciples would betray him. He could have reacted in anger, demanding total loyalty. He did not. He showed only love toward each, including Judas, by washing their feet.

## SIGNS OF SERVANTHOOD

In Jesus' day the roads of Palestine were dusty and muddy. The sandals that were worn did not keep dirt off the feet. Most houses and buildings had basins of water at the entrance. Often there was a servant with a towel present to greet guests and wash their feet. Jesus and his disciples had no such servants. They had to perform these tasks among themselves. Jesus' action was to take a custom and reinterpret it. While it was customary to wash feet before a meal, it was usually done by a servant, certainly not one regarded as rabbi or teacher.

The story of Jesus washing the disciples' feet is not found in any Gospel but the Gospel of John. However, the event continues to capture the hearts of Christian people who find within it a profound call to be involved in various ministries of love and service. The towel and basin is a symbol often seen on paraments and liturgical garments representing the servanthood of the church. In The United Methodist Church, this symbol signifies the ministry of the diaconate.

## Footwashing May Symbolize the Crucifixion

At first Peter refused to allow Jesus to wash his feet (8). Jesus told Peter that unless he allowed his feet to be washed, he could have no part of Jesus. The footwashing may symbolize the forthcoming death of Jesus, so similar is this response of Peter (8-9) to Mark 8:31-33. In comparison to

his earlier objections, Peter became willing to have not only his feet, but all of his body washed! He wanted more than a small share of Jesus.

Verse 10 may refer to the Jewish ritual of purification. If this ritual had been done, obviously one was clean. Footwashing was all that remained when arriving for dinner. The phrase, "except for the feet," was omitted in some Bible manuscripts.

## Footwashing May Symbolize Christian Baptism

Peter and the disciples were already washed or cleansed by Jesus. Jesus had already forgiven them and received their allegiance. Some scholars understand this passage to refer to baptism. They argue that when one entered a house in Palestine, one washed the feet. When one enters the Christian community, one is "washed" in baptism. If one is bathed already in the cleansing power of the cross, one need only wash symbolically, marking the entry into the community of believers.

## Footwashing May Symbolize Christian Servanthood

The Christian community, for which this Gospel was originally written, may have practiced footwashing. If so, undoubtedly it did so as a reminder that love and service is the task of the Christian. Jesus as teacher and Lord has served as a model of what the disciples should do (verses 12-17). Verse 17 (called a beatitude) states that if you know this, then blessed are you if you do this. To know love in this way is to act on it and in doing so to receive a blessing.

What happened when Jesus showed his supreme love in this humble act? He was immediately betrayed in self-serving greed, a direct contrast to his selfless giving. In the upper room (18) Jesus acknowledged that one would betray him. Quoting from Psalm 41:9,

"Even my bosom friend in whom I trusted,
who ate of my bread, has lifted the heel against me."

This psalm is a lament, a prayer for healing in sickness. The psalmist lamented the disdain shown toward the sick; even his best friend had turned against him. In the ancient Middle East, to break bread with some-one was a sign of friendship and loyalty. To "lift up the heel" against someone, implied violence, perhaps a kicking or a bludgeoning, like an animal attacking the hand that feeds it.

Jesus knew about the betrayal and warned the disciples. It was bound to happen. John was clear here and elsewhere (10:17-18) that Jesus was not in a situation from which he could not escape. Jesus was in control throughout his ministry, to the very end.

## Judas the Traitor

Simon Peter, in verse 23 asked "the disciple whom Jesus loved" who was sitting close to Jesus, to find out the identity of the betrayer. Actually the position at the table was more of a reclining one. Jesus dipped a morsel and handed it to Judas, and with this gesture indicated that Judas was the one. In spite of Jesus' appeal to love, the text records that Satan entered into Judas. He was closed off to any further appeal from Jesus. "Do quickly what you are going to do" (27), Jesus told him. Jesus, in shunning his garment in an act of servanthood, peeled away the covering revealing the hypocrisy of Judas. Judas, ashamed, fled in the night.

Nicodemus had come to Jesus under the cover of darkness. Judas left Jesus under the cover of darkness, only to return again in the shadows of the garden to betray him. The disciples may have thought Judas had been instructed to take the money and buy food for the feast or to give the customary offering to the poor (29).

## Peter, the "Devoted Denier"

In this passage there is, on the one hand, the complete betrayal of Judas; on the other hand, one finds the misunderstanding and disloyalty of Simon Peter. Simon Peter asked Jesus where he was going (36). Jesus responded that it was to a place where Peter could not immediately go. Later, Peter would be able to follow (36). There is a tradition that says Peter later took a similar path as did his Savior. He died, according to the story, a martyr, hung upside down on a cross in mockery of his faith.

Peter boastfully assured Jesus of his loyalty (37). In verse 38, however, Jesus predicted that his self-assured disciple would deny him three times before morning. (Cockcrow occurred between 12 and 3 A.M.)

Judas' departure brought about the hour that the Son of man was glorified through the cross (31-32). Through Jesus God was glorified. This passage began Jesus' farewell to his disciples. He was going where they could not go. He gave them the new commandment to love one another (34) as he loved them. Their love would demonstrate who they were. Love would give them their identity. People would know they were disciples by their love. Love would be their acts of serving. The early church observed Holy Thursday or "Maundy Thursday," a term taken from the Latin word for commandment associated with this verse.

73

One thing that is striking about this passage is that John did not record the institution of Holy Communion or Eucharist as the other Gospels did. Why did he not tell of the passing of the bread and cup? Several answers to that question have been offered. Perhaps it was because he felt that his discussion of the bread of life in chapter 6 was sufficient. John may have been even more interested in getting across the commandment to love one another, to demonstrate the meaning of the Eucharist as an act of cleansing love. It has been suggested that John was secretive about the Eucharist, because it was not revealed to new Christians until after they were baptized. Or, it may have been that John assumed his readers would already know about the Eucharist and felt no particular need to repeat the story. Instead, he focused on the foot-washing and the betrayal. John gave us the loving, sacrificial example of Jesus, the dark demonic Judas, and the devoted one who denied Jesus, Peter.

## Dimension 3:
## What Does the Bible Mean to Us?

There are several meaningful elements in this passage. Primary is the love of Jesus. Jesus loves us to the end. Such love is symbolized well when one takes up a towel and a basin to perform an act of service. The lesson is twofold: Jesus serves us and Jesus teaches us how to serve others. Many times we focus on the latter. It may be easier in some ways to serve others rather than to receive and accept service from another.

> Feet are not one of the more revered or dignified parts of the human body. Ugly, awkward, and smelly, feet take a beating. In Jesus' day feet were the dirtiest part of the body.

Yes, Jesus exemplified what we are to do. But we are to be served as well as to serve. Jesus serves us as he did the disciples, by cleansing us, by submitting to the cross—an act which cleansed humankind.

Jesus did not shun the ugly and the dirty parts of life. He simply cleaned away the dirt. He does that also for us. In doing so we are shown how to clean up the figurative dirt of this world—the waste of injustice, the mire of deceit and pride, the dust of destruction and violence.

### The Greatness of Service

Did Jesus mean we are to literally wash each others' feet? Is the Christian church to practice footwashing? A few denominations practice footwashing as an act of worship to symbolically empower people to go out and serve. In today's world, with the shoes and footwear normally worn, the practice that Jesus used to illustrate humble, sacrificial service seems rather foreign to us. There is no need for special attentions to be given to washing feet. Ultimately, however, we may want to look beyond the actual act to the radical intent behind the act. Jesus showed us how to serve others. Our task is to find new forms of servanthood that would exemplify this same intense love.

The most mundane service can be a way of ministry. One forty-one-year-old woman in the throes of building a solid career as an attorney took on the task of caring for her older sister—a stroke victim—performing even the most menial tasks with her. In doing so she reported a renewed bond of friendship with her sister and an increased experience of love and spiritual growth. She modeled for her family and friends the sacrificial love that Christians are called to demonstrate.

The one true greatness in the world is the greatness of service. The New Testament carries a strong tradition that Jesus reversed the ordinary measure of greatness. Yet, even in the church there is grappling for position and power. The church is not immune to human failings. Given that, we still can practice humility and service and witness many examples of such in the church today.

## The Image of a Servant

The image of the servant is not as simple or straightforward as it may sound. Jesus did not intend that those involved in service should become doormats. A news documentary reported the story of a black South African woman who, for twenty years, walked five miles to work and five miles home each day. For those twenty years she worked for a white woman who did not even know her correct name. For twenty years she had called the woman by the wrong name.

Jesus did not intend service to be a form of oppression. True servanthood is *chosen*, taken up as a response to God's love.

> Can we see ourselves giving up the ordinary, self-centered power struggle and taking up the greatest power of all—the power that comes from serving others in the name of Christ?

The image of the servant is made clearer to us by the contrasting image of betrayer. Like Judas before us, our choice is to serve Christ or to betray him. Judas was in a position of honor among the disciples. Yet, he deserted Jesus. Literally, Judas "sold out." Jesus' spirit was troubled, we are told, as deeply as when Lazarus died. It was a terrible loss. We, too, are friends of Jesus. For a friend to turn away is even more painful than the attack of an enemy. If we turn away from Jesus, it is a terrible loss.

We know how it feels to be betrayed by a friend. One can hardly go through life without having this experience in one form or another. By contrast, Jesus does not forsake us. He does not "take the money and run." He does not leave us impoverished.

Why did Judas do it? Was it greed, pride, a psychological disorder, or the sheer fact of being possessed by Satan? In any case, the disciples, in asking who it would be, seemed to indicate that it could have been any one of them. Undoubtedly, we all have within us the potential to betray. When Satan entered Judas, the light of Christ was shut off. We may not usually speak of being possessed by Satan today, but to be closed off from Christ is equal to such. It is to stumble out into the night as Judas did.

## Jesus Commands Love

Even with the risk of betrayal, Jesus commanded us to love one another as he loved. *Commandment* may be a rather strong word when speaking of love. We often think of love as an emotion over which we have no control. But Jesus *commands* love; the love he commanded is more of an action than an emotion. We can choose to take up this commandment to love. In doing so we will be identified by our love. As the song goes, "They will know we are Christians by our love."

In John, particularly in this passage, we are permitted a glimpse into the mind and heart of Simon Peter. Peter had a unique relationship with Jesus indicated by the new name Jesus gave him (1:42). As his name was new, so would be his life through knowing Jesus. We can relate to Peter's desire to go with Jesus. Perhaps, like him, we have failed to comprehend the vastness of Jesus' love for us. We are devoted to Jesus, but do we deny him as well? Peter, in many ways, is every Christian. Our faith has its ups and downs. One minute we are willing to lay down our lives, the next we act like we do not even know him. Jesus loved Peter for all his faults and he loves us as well. This chapter ends as it began—telling of the most wondrous love that is beyond all telling.

## Dimension 4:
## A Daily Bible Journey Plan

*Day 1:* **John 13:1**

*Day 2:* **John 13:2-11**

*Day 3:* **John 13:12-17**

*Day 4:* **John 13:18-20**

*Day 5:* **John 13:21-30**

*Day 6:* **John 13:31-35**

*Day 7:* **John 13:36-38**

# 10

# THE ADVOCATE WILL COME

## What to Watch For

Many of the timeless teachings of chapters 14–16 will be familiar to us.
Still, they challenge and evoke response. Chapter 14 begins with a word of
comfort. Jesus must go away, but he would not leave his followers home-
less and orphaned. He would prepare a place for them. As you read, watch
for these emphases:

➤ Jesus spoke to them of the Advocate that would come. The first
promise of the gift of the Holy Spirit in this Gospel comes in 14:16.
Other promises of the Spirit are given in 14:26, 15:26, and 16:7. John
stressed that the Spirit would come to teach and to help them remember
and continue the work of Jesus.
➤ Jesus spoke to his followers of the peace that he would leave them. It
was a peace that would drive out fear.
➤ Jesus told his followers that he was returning to God. If they truly loved
him, they would rejoice.
➤ Jesus spoke of his victory over the ruler of the world. Though his death
may look like defeat, he assured them that the ruler of the world would
have no power over him.
➤ Jesus spoke of his love for God and directed his followers to rise and go.

Chapters 15 and 16 continue the farewell discourse.

1. What will the promised Advocate do according to verse 26?

2. How will Jesus comfort the disciples in view of his going away?

3. Why did Jesus say the disciples should rejoice?

4. What did Jesus say to them regarding the ruler of the world?

### The Farewell Discourse

The material beginning in 13:31 has been described as the "last discourse" or "farewell discourse" of Jesus. Actually it is several discourses. John may have meant the farewell addresses often given by acclaimed persons in literature just prior to their deaths. Other examples of farewell addresses in the Bible include Jacob's farewell beginning in Genesis 47:29 and Moses' numerous farewell speeches in Deuteronomy. The other Gospels also contain final discourses of Jesus, but they focus on different matters than does John, such as the destruction of the Temple and the coming of the Son of man (Mark 13; Matthew 24; Luke 21).

Chapter fourteen recalls words of comfort and compassion shared with the disciples on the advent of Jesus' death. The Twelve were told about his death ahead of time and were forewarned not to interpret it as a defeat. Indeed, it would be a victory! They should rejoice! Jesus provided them with a way to understand his death. They might not initially understand, but later they would.

## The Legacy of Jesus

The particular passage of 14:25-31 is sometimes referred to as the legacy of Jesus. He would be leaving something behind. He would leave the promise of the Advocate and he would leave peace. The word John used, *Parakleos* (or *Paraclete* in the English spelling) means literally "one called" (*kletos*) "to be alongside" (*para*). It has been translated various ways: Comforter, Advocate, Counselor, Champion, Helper. The sense is that this is a presence that would be with, or alongside, the followers. The *Paraclete* is then named the Holy Spirit. In John 14:16, we read that the Spirit would be sent upon Jesus' request. In 14:26 the Spirit would be sent by God in Jesus' name. Note the importance of the phrase "in my name," implying a connection, a union, with Jesus. The Spirit would represent Jesus, when he no longer would be physically seen by his followers. The phrase "in my name" occurs seven times, perhaps indicating that the Spirit will "perfect" the Christian community, leading it in ways beyond that which followers have known with Jesus. Jesus has authorized the Spirit's work. The followers of Jesus would not have to rely solely on their memories of him. They would not be alone; he would be with them through the Spirit.

## FUNCTIONS OF THE ADVOCATE

- To be with you, abide in you (14:17);
- To teach you everything (14:26);
- To remind you of all that I have said to you (14:26);
- To testify on my behalf (15:26);
- To prove the world wrong, to show the error of the world about sin, righteousness, and judgment (16:7-8)).

The phrase to "teach you everything" does not imply that Jesus left something out in his own teaching, but rather that the Spirit will enable persons to understand the meaning of Jesus' teachings more fully. The Spirit will teach everything that Christians need to know. The Spirit will serve as a guide through life. The Spirit will also help Christians remember what Jesus said and did so that his mission will be continued. The Spirit offers consolation and challenge, encouragement and peacemaking.

These verses about the Holy Spirit were significant in the formation of the doctrine of the Trinity during the fourth century when it became necessary to clarify the nature of the relation between God, Jesus Christ, and the Holy Spirit.

## No Vague Presence

John's conception of the Spirit is rooted in the Old Testament understanding of the Spirit of God. That Spirit was the source of life, a creating power (Genesis 1:2; 2:7; 6:3). The Spirit of God came upon the prophets as they spoke for God (Joel 2:28). The Spirit of God also had a role in bringing about the coming of the Messiah. The Spirit is not simply a vague presence but has well defined purposes. The Holy Spirit is also called the Spirit of truth in John 14:17. It is a guide for truth, helping one to be truthful and to know the truth of Jesus Christ.

Verse 26 spoke of two of the functions of the Spirit. The Advocate whom the Father will send will "teach you everything" and "remind you of all that I have said to you."

## Jesus Grants Shalom

Verse 27 offers additional words of comfort to those extended in 14:1. Yet these words are not sugar-coated, benign expressions of "do not worry." They carry with them a challenge: "Peace I leave with you; my peace I give to you." The challenge to the individual Christian is to accept the gift. The gift of peace is not the absence of conflict, for Jesus and the disciples were facing much conflict and turmoil. It is more an attitude of trust. The human tendency, exemplified in the disciples, is not to trust, to be sceptical. The peace of Christ remains solid during storms and crises. The things of the world do not affect it. Followers of Jesus can know *shalom*.

The disciples expressed concern over Jesus' departure. Jesus responded to their concern in verse 28, reminding the Twelve that they should rejoice that he was going to God. The phrase "if you loved me" did not indicate that the disciples did not love Jesus. John knew that they did. Despite having love, they were possessive and possibly a bit selfish. The kind of love Jesus was talking about was the kind that could recognize that Jesus was serving God's purpose. The thought is carried further in 16:7: "It is to your advantage that I go away." Rather than be afraid because of their own insecurities, they should trust in the security Christ gave them and rejoice.

The last clause of verse 28, "because the Father is greater than I" has sparked much debate. Jesus attempted to reassure the disciples by saying they should rejoice because he was going to one who was greater than he. This phrase has been called upon to deny the divinity of Jesus. It was central in the Arian controversy of the fourth century. It is a confusing phrase, particularly since John 10:30 has Jesus saying: "The Father and I are one." The phrase "because the Father is greater than I" expresses the distinction between Jesus and the Father. Some scholars have interpreted it to mean that while Jesus was on earth, he was less than the Father. As indicated above, Jesus' teachings were not intended to explain the nature of the Trinity. Such seeming contradictions did not concern John. The formal theological explanations came in the centuries after John wrote. Perhaps the implication is that the Son is not more important and does not supercede the one who sent him.

> Arianism taught that Jesus was lesser than God.

## Sorrow Turned to Joy

Jesus told them about his death before it happened so that they might exercise the peace of Christ. Instead of being shattered, their faith could be strengthened. In the closing remarks of this passage, Jesus pointed out that he would not talk much more. Yet the discourse continues for two to three more chapters!

The themes discussed in these chapters are similar to themes in chapters 13 and 14. Other scholars see it as a natural, intended break. Jesus told them he would be going soon and the ruler of the world would be coming. Satan was coming to work to set his death in motion. There would be a struggle with the ruler of the world. Satan had no power over Jesus, however. Satan did not cause Jesus to die in that sense. Jesus' death was caused by his obedience to God. Jesus knew he would be victorious. Jesus' obedience to God meant that the ruler of the world could not gain any power over him.

> It has been suggested that these chapters were somehow rearranged and later material added or moved. In this schema, scholars suggest that chapter 18 may have followed immediately chapter 14 by "echoing" the words of 14:1-3 and projecting ahead to Jesus' arrest. Chapters 15–17 may have been added later, perhaps by the original author of this Gospel or by others in the community of faith.

In doing as he had been commanded, Jesus would show the world how much he loved God. Verse 31 is the only direct statement in the Gospels of Jesus' love for his heavenly parent. That love was an action. It was doing what God had commanded. He was modeling that love for us.

Jesus asked all present to rise and leave the place where they had eaten supper. Jesus' directive to get up and be going was also given in Mark

14:42 at Gethsemane. Some have speculated that since chapter 15 continued the discourse, the directive was not a literal one, but a summons to the disciples to prepare themselves mentally and emotionally for what was to take place. It may also be that they did leave and go to the garden where Jesus used the vine and branches growing there to make a point. Or, as mentioned, there may have been some rearranging of the text. In chapters 15 and 16 Jesus called himself the true vine and spoke of the "branching out" of his mission despite the "hatred of the world" and persecution. In the message that he was leaving, Jesus offered hope and consolation. The sorrow of the disciples would soon turn to joy!

## Dimension 3:
## What Does the Bible Mean to Us?

### The Promise of the Advocate

This passage tells us of the promise to send the Advocate, the Holy Spirit. "Advocate" is an intriguing, appealing translation of *Parakleos*. Everyone needs an advocate, a champion, at some point in life. It is important to have someone "on our side." This will be one function of the Holy Spirit, we are told—to be an advocate, a helper, for those who follow Christ and continue his mission. Do we think of the Holy Spirit in this way? Do we view the Holy Spirit as our counselor, guide, advocate, helper?

Sometimes the Holy Spirit is thought of as something magical, a kind of mysterious providence that makes things go right and fall into place for Christians. The message of John regarding the Holy Spirit offers a challenge to that view.

Modern minds may resist talking of the Holy Spirit as something ghostlike and unreal. John challenges that view by providing concrete explanations of just what the Holy Spirit is and does.

### THE HOLY SPIRIT GUIDES

The Greek word for spirit is *pneuma,* a translation of the Hebrew word *ruah*. Both mean "wind" or "breath." The metaphor implied in the word describes the presence of one who surrounds us, one we feel but cannot see, one, who in a sailing sense, takes us to our destination. An old Irish blessing has a line in it: "May the wind blow at your back." In other words may you be guided forward instead of backward.

## The Holy Spirit Teaches

One function of the Advocate is to teach. The Christian will be by definition always one who is taught, a learner. This function defies the guardian angel/rescuer view of the Spirit. Why do we need more teaching? Because new situations and experiences require continued interpretation and application of the Christian message. This may be an injunction against arrogant self-satisfaction. No Christian knows all there is to know. Each has something to learn from another.

To teach is to guide. We may resist that guidance, but we all need it. Guidance is not advice. It is not telling us what we should do. It is helping us to be the person we need to be, in order to do what God wants us to do.

Sometimes to teach is to confront. The Holy Spirit as teacher confronts our worldly misconceptions, confronts our moral failures, and confronts the failures of our faith. Do we think of the Holy Spirit as our teacher? This is probably an underrated understanding of the Spirit. If the Holy Spirit is our teacher, human teachers are representative witnesses of the message guided by the Spirit. Do we look upon the teachers in our church this way?

## The Spirit Helps Us Remember the Teachings of Jesus

The Holy Spirit will recall to us what Jesus has said and help us get at the meaning of his teachings. Recalling or remembering is a fundamental activity of Christians. Many of us who are nurtured into the Christian faith from a young age probably cannot remember a time when we did not hear the stories of the faith. We may have been hearing the stories of Jesus before we were yet two years of age. All our lives we remember, and retell those stories. Those of us who became Christians later in life jump into the middle of the remembering activity. It did not take long to hear some of the Bible stories and sayings of Jesus, and to participate fully in the remembering. The coming of the Advocate assures the living presence of Jesus in all Christians, teaching us and helping us remember.

## The Holy Spirit Sanctifies

The Holy Spirit is one aspect of the Trinity, our attempt to describe the completeness of God. We may know and experience God as a personal power of love and goodness in the world. That power is a personal power. It is a creating power. God has created and continues to create. It is also a redeeming power. That power exemplified in Christ redeems us from the enemy of sin. That power is a sanctifying power, working in us to

Some traditions speak of "getting the Spirit." In John, the emphasis was on the sending of the Spirit as a gift for the benefit of all rather than on the grasping of the Spirit by particular individuals. There was no reliable step-by-step guide on how to get the Spirit, because it does not work that way. God gives the Spirit, and, like salvation, we cannot buy it or earn it.

increase our faith and bring us close to God and one another. The work of the Spirit is sometimes called sanctification.

The Holy Spirit continues to shape our bond with Jesus Christ and the bond formed by loving one another as directed in 13:34. This is the basis for the carrying on of Jesus' mission for the church. When something goes wrong in the church, the bond of love may be called upon to address it. Guided by the Spirit, we ask the question of what love requires us to do. The answers may not be of one mind or voice, in fact probably will not be. The Spirit may certainly be communicated in more than one voice.

## The Holy Spirit Brings Shalom

Jesus spoke of the gift of the Holy Spirit. The magnitude of that gift is difficult to comprehend and fully appreciate. He gave then to those he left behind the gift of peace, *shalom*. We too, experience separation from Jesus, the separation of time, presence, and understanding. We are recipients of the gift of the peace of Christ. No greater gift has ever been given. It is the ability to trust, to put away fear in times of trouble. With all the hassles and chaos of life, we sometimes cry, "If I could just get some peace around here." The peace of Christ is the realization that our worldly failures, or even successes, are not the ultimate end. The worries or problems that we have do not mean that God is not with us, abiding with us. God is there through it all. The peace Jesus was talking about is the understanding and knowledge and heartfelt experience of this *shalom*.

### Dimension 4:
### A Daily Bible Journey Plan

*Day 1:* John 14:1-24
*Day 2:* John 14:25-31
*Day 3:* John 15:1-11
*Day 4:* John 15:12-27
*Day 5:* John 16:1-15
*Day 6:* John 16:16-24
*Day 7:* John 16:25-33

# 11

# 𝒯HE HOUR HAS COME

## What to Watch For

The last discourse comes to a close. John records Jesus' beautiful prayer for his followers in chapter 17. In chapter 18 we are told that Jesus and his disciples went to a garden, located across the Kidron valley, east of Jerusalem. Crossing the Kidron valley, one comes to the Mount of Olives. Judas appeared, leading a detachment of soldiers and Temple police to arrest Jesus. The arresting force may have expected trouble for they came armed and carrying torches.

All four Gospels record the betrayal and arrest of Jesus. The Gospels differ on some important details. As you read this passage, watch for these emphases:

➤ John emphasized that Jesus stepped forward to meet them. His hour had come. He did not attempt to hide or escape.
➤ Peter tried to resist by drawing his sword and cutting off the ear of Malchus, the servant of the high priest. Jesus, however, stopped Peter.
➤ The soldiers arrested and bound Jesus, taking him first to Annas, a former high priest, and then to Caiaphas, the incumbent high priest, for questioning.

This section from John begins what is known as the "Passion narrative." In this narrative, John shared not only the deep suffering of Jesus, or the final act of human rejection, but also Jesus' triumph over suffering.

1. Where did Jesus and his disciples go after the prayer in chapter 17?

2. What was Judas' role in the event?

3. How did Jesus react to the presence of the soldiers and what was his stipulation?

4. How did Simon Peter react in the situation?

5. What did the soldiers do with Jesus?

### Jesus Crossed the Kidron Valley

After the meal in the upper room, Jesus prayed for himself, for his disciples, and for those who believed in him. John 18:1 is a transition to the Passion story. The Kidron valley had played important roles in the history of the Jewish people. Years before Jesus crossed the valley en route to his death, David had fled across the valley during Absalom's rebellion (2 Samuel 15:23). Nine centuries later, Jesus crossed the valley with his disciples, coming finally to a garden somewhere near the Mount of Olives.

The passover lambs were killed in the Temple and the blood was poured on the altar. There was a channel from the altar to the Kidron where the blood was drained. John's report that Jesus crossed here may have symbolized that Jesus was the ultimate sacrificial lamb, a theme begun in chapter 13.

Judas assumed that Jesus would go to the garden after the meal. It was a favorite retreat for Jesus and the disciples.

### Differences Among the Gospels

While John's account is similar to the other Gospels, there are some striking differences. Getting at these differences helps us understand the particular message John wanted to convey.

In Mark 14:33 and Matthew 26:37, Jesus took only the three favored disciples with him—Peter, James, and John. Luke and John have all the disciples present. Why? Perhaps for John, the more witnesses, the better. John stressed that Jesus did not resist. It would have been possible for him to have resisted with more than a few present, but he chose to go forward freely. Judas told the authorities where Jesus could be arrested at night in a secluded area without danger of attracting the attention of the crowds that usually followed Jesus.

Another difference between John and the Synoptics is that John was the only one who had Roman soldiers present. Mark and Matthew may imply that Pilate knew and consented to the arrest. Most readers assume these were Roman soldiers because John also stated that the officers of the chief priests (the Sadducees) and the Pharisees came as well. These represented all the leading Jewish authorities. John had both the Jews and the Romans going after Jesus, but he did not say which group initiated the arrest or bore more responsibility. There is a wide spectrum of positions on the involvement of the Jews, ranging from complete responsibility for Jesus' death, to partial responsibility shared with the Romans, to no real responsibility.

> The text says he led a *speira*, a detachment, a band or cohort that could have meant as many as six hundred soldiers (or a smaller, representative group).

Why did John give the picture of a large group coming to arrest Jesus? It may have been that John wished to show that the Sanhedrin wanted Roman support or vice versa. So many troops may imply that the authorities suspected that Jesus had formed a small guerrilla force outside the city. The large number may also be symbolic of the hostile world from all sides against Jesus, though this is not expressly obvious from the text. John possibly made a connection with those who had come to arrest him before (7:30, 44; 8:20, 59; 10:39; 12:36b), with those who were not able to arrest him because his hour had not come. Now they were able to do what they had tried to do before. The detachment was something of a lynch mob. They brought lanterns and torches, expecting to have to search for Jesus. They did not have to hunt for him. He came out to meet them. We may assume that the fourth evangelist intended the irony of using torches and lanterns to search for the Light of the World.

John differed from the Synoptics in that John did not paint a scene of agony in the garden of Gethsemane. It has been suggested that John did not recount the scene because he felt such troubling thoughts would not have been present in an already glorified Jesus. (Jesus was glorified in 13:31.) The picture of Jesus as troubled about his fate did not suit John's purposes. He understood that Jesus willingly went out to meet his opponents. He freely laid his life down. Interestingly, this emphasis in John has been explained as an attempt to dispel the argument that Jesus, if he was divine, should have saved himself.

Jesus asked the soldiers, "Whom are you looking for?" (4) This was practically the same question asked in 1:38, his first words of the Gospel spoken to the first disciples Andrew and Simon Peter. The term "Jesus of Nazareth" could have been a reference to his hometown, as it appears to identify him; or it could have been a kind of "put down" (Nazareth was not a booming metropolis). It may have been simply a title identifying his claim to be Messiah.

## "I Am He"

Jesus answered, "I am he," *ego eimi* in the Greek, which meant both "I am the one you seek" and may have been the divine name of "I am who I am," which the Lord spoke to Moses at the burning bush. Possibly Jesus' words were recalling the "I am he" from Isaiah 43. Regardless, the soldiers "fell to the ground." Why?

Several possibilities exist. The soldiers may have been so awed and overcome by Jesus that they fell back. It may have been merely a normal reaction, revealing that Jews prostrated themselves upon hearing the name of God. Falling down was also a reaction to divine revelation in Daniel 2:46; 8:18; and Revelation 1:17. Another possibility is that John may also have had in mind Psalm 27:2, which stated that evildoers will stumble and fall.

Jesus repeated his question to the soldiers, and they repeated they were looking for Jesus of Nazareth. Again, Jesus identified himself, but he stipulated that his followers not be harmed. The divine name was used to protect his followers. Jesus knew that if he were being charged with treason or blasphemy, those with him could be charged as accessories to his crimes. He wanted to assure, as stated in verse 9, that none that had been given to him were lost. His intercession on behalf of his disciples recalled the prayer he had just prayed for them, especially 17:12 where he spoke of his protection and care of the disciples.

## Peter Attempted to Resist the Arrest

Verse 10 told how Peter cut off the ear of Malchus. All of the Gospels relate the incident of the cutting off of the soldier's ear, but only John names the persons involved. The victim was a servant of the high priest and not a soldier. Why did John name them? Some commentators attributed it to the tendency to embellish stories with details such as names, dates, and places over time to give credibility to the account. The problem with this explanation is that the tendency was to name well-known persons to gain such plausibility. Malchus was a common name in that era, but he was unknown. In the Gospel of John the cutting of the ear is not an occasion for a miraculous healing as it is in Luke 22:51, but an opportunity for Jesus to demonstrate again that he was in charge of what happened, that he would "drink the cup" he had been given. Peter tried to defend his leader, but Jesus did not need defending. Peter tried to resist the arrest by the power of the sword, which contrasted with Jesus' peaceful approach in submitting to arrest.

## The High Priest Questions Jesus

First the arresting force took Jesus to the house of Annas, then to Caiaphas. Why would they take him to Annas when Caiaphas was the high priest? Annas was a former high priest from the year A.D. 6 to 15. According to historian Josephus, he was a powerful and wealthy man appointed by Quirinius. Four or five of his sons also became high priests. He was Caiaphas' father-in-law as well. It may have been that he retained his honorific title or that Caiaphas was a Roman appointee and Annas was recognized as the true high priest. John again noted Caiaphas' unconscious prophecy.

At one time a high priest served for life; when the Romans came into power, the office was corrupt and given to the highest bidder. (See the notes on Caiaphas in session 7 of this study, page 57).

John omitted an appearance of Jesus before the entire Sanhedrin, which the Synoptics included. John did not describe any real charges or actions taken against Jesus at the trial. He had previously mentioned that it had already been decided that Jesus must die (11:49-51). John was not concerned with the details of a trial. It has been pointed out that the proceedings of the Sanhedrin as described in the Gospels violate the code in the

*Mishnah*, the written collection of rabbinic laws. For example, a night meeting on the eve of a holy day would not be in accordance with the code. Also in the code, two sessions were required for a death penalty. John 18:31 stated that the Sanhedrin could not execute the death

penalty. It is not known whether these laws were operative in Jesus' time. According to Jewish law, no accused person is required to testify when, to do so, one might incriminate oneself. Annas violated this code according to the account that follows in 18:19-24.

Throughout these chapters John maintained that Jesus, in not resisting, was truly in control—despite the ridicule, the questioning, the physical abuse. These chapters describe the fulfillment of the glorification of the Son given by God. The glorified Son would "drink the cup" intended by God. Chapter 18 continues with Peter's denial, first to a woman gatekeeper, then to those at the bonfire, and then to a slave. Jesus was questioned and brought before Pilate, who tried to release him for the Passover. He was overruled by the mob who cried, "not this man, but Barabbas" (40).

## Dimension 3:
## What Does the Bible Mean to Us?

### Scripture Continues to Reveal Its Treasures

Some may think the story of Jesus' arrest, crucifixion, and resurrection has become so familiar, by being read and dramatized so often, that it does not deserve study. Some Bible students wonder what more could possibly be said or learned that has not already been taught. In truth, there are layers of meaning yet to be uncovered in the biblical texts. The depth of meaning of this material has yet to be exhausted, and persons continue to find help in this Gospel in making their faith relevant to new situations. The perspective of John is of one looking back. Those who were not present can see and understand through the eyes of tradition.

> In our time we engage in what Plato called *anamnesis* or "searching memory" for signs of God's relation to humanity. We scan the tradition, applying it to our lives. In this way, then, even though it was a once-and-for-all event, the Passion narrative happens over and over for us.

Upon hearing this text we can feel the hostility of the mob that came to arrest Jesus. We know what it feels like to be under attack. We have all been faced with hostility. Several theorists have identified that we live in a time that is hostile to Christianity. The problem may not so much be of the world coming after Christians with torches and weapons, but the world simply dismissing Christianity as irrelevant and unnecessary. Stephen Carter in *The Culture of Disbelief* explores a culture come of age that was raised not to believe in anything, and he describes how this affects the world. Some have even called our time "a spiritual wilderness." The portrait of Jesus painted in John, however, is of one who—despite hostility, or indifference—stood firm, did not hide who he was, and came forth in courage.

In this passage we have the two extremes of human reaction in Judas and Peter. On the one hand we have the traitor—the one who knew Jesus, yet ultimately was given over to evil to take sides against him. We have dealt with the devastating effects of betrayal on humanity in this study. When times get tough, there is always the temptation to jump ship.

## Peter Attempted to Save His Savior

Then on the other hand we have Peter, who, in keeping with his character, reacted to try to resist what was happening, to "save" Jesus as if he needed to be saved. His violent action was in sharp contrast to Jesus' peaceful and calm approach. Peter served here as an instrument for a unique insight into Jesus. Jesus did not act defensively. There was no mounting of an attack. Jesus' passive resistance has inspired many of the great human rights advocates of modern times such as Ghandi and Martin Luther King, Jr. Jesus voluntarily turned himself in and requested the safety of his followers as he had done when he prayed in chapter 17.

Back to Peter. We may think Peter foolish and impetuous, or we may admire him for his courage in attempting to protect Jesus. There are times that do seem to call for one to defend or even assert oneself. Peter may have been what popular "psycho-babble" terms a "fixer." He wanted to fix the situation, turn it around, make it right. The world is full of fixers. We "fixers" insist that things work out a certain way. We are uncompromising. We will resort to extreme measures to rescue a situation. We misuse power. We are defensive, and we are not above revenge if it suits our purposes. In several other occasions in the Gospels, the disciples wanted revenge on those who opposed Jesus. In anger, Peter struck an unarmed man and cut off his ear. It seems to be a natural, human inclination to strike back, to "get even." Again, Jesus' behavior serves as a model. In his supreme obedience he would drink the cup given by God. Our love and obedience to God as Christians can guide our actions and responses when we are threatened. Jesus had reportedly asked for the cup to be removed from him according to Mark 14:36. Not so in John. Here he willingly drinks the cup. For Peter and for us it is a hard lesson to learn to accept the cup, to forebear and not try to fix things that cannot be fixed. It is difficult for us to accept that God is in control and not us. In the Gospel of John, Jesus was in complete con-

> Jesus' intercession on behalf of others is an important model for Christians. We too are called to make intercession for others. Intercessory prayer has been practiced by Christians for centuries. It involves petitioning God with particular needs. It is not that God does not know our needs and must be "reminded." In intercessory prayer we vocalize and name the needs of our community and in doing so align our needs and wills more closely to God's.

> The cup symbolizes suffering in the Gospels. (See Matthew 20:23; 26:29.)

91

trol because of his complete obedience to God. Sometimes control is sub-mission. Henri Nouwen once wrote in *Reaching Out*, "It takes only a hostile word to make us feel sad and lonely. It takes only a rejecting gesture to plunge us into self-complaint. It takes only a substantial failure in our work to lead us into a self-destructive depression. . . . We have become victimized by our surrounding world suggesting to us that we are 'in control.' "

We are really only in control when we relinquish ourselves to the control of God. We, too, can "drink the cup" given to us. The cup of suffering is also the cup of salvation. Of course suffering is to be alleviated whenever and wherever possible. Yet suffering is a part of human life and to participate in it, as Jesus did, is to suffer at one time or another. The wonderful, uplifting message of John is that suffering is not ultimate. We are told, "Your pain will turn into joy. . .your hearts will rejoice."

## Dimension 4:
## A Daily Bible Journey Plan

*Day 1:*  **John 17:1-5**

*Day 2:*  **John 17:6-19**

*Day 3:*  **John 17:20-26**

*Day 4:*  **John 18:1-14**

*Day 5:*  **John 18:15-18**

*Day 6:*  **John 18:19-27**

*Day 7:*  **John 18:28-40**

# 12

# $\mathcal{J}$T Is
# FINISHED

## *What to Watch For*

John wrote of the Crucifixion sparing little of the agony. As you read this passage, watch for the following emphases:

➤ Jesus was sent to Pilate's headquarters. Pilate debated with the Jews and with himself over Jesus' guilt. He tried to get a plea of innocence accepted, but failed. Pilate, in mockery, had Jesus flogged and adorned with the clothing of a king. Still, the religious leaders demanded that he be crucified. Pilate questioned Jesus in private, trying to understand what he could have done. Jesus did not grovel, nor plead for his life. Pilate gave in and handed him over to be crucified.

➤ Jesus carried his own cross to Golgotha where he was crucified between two others. The sign "Jesus of Nazareth, the King of the Jews" was attached to the cross. The Jews protested, but Pilate refused to change what he had written.

➤ John described how the soldiers divided Jesus' clothes among them.

➤ Some women were at the cross and the "disciple whom he loved" (26). According to John, Jesus told his mother to accept the disciple as her son. He told the disciple to consider Mary his mother (27).

➤ Jesus expressed thirst. A sponge of sour wine was lifted up to him.

➤ Each of these things served to fulfill the Scripture. (See also John 13:18; 17:12; Psalm 69:21.) Jesus said, "It is finished." He gave up his spirit.

1. What happened to Jesus when he was handed over to be crucified?

2. What was Pilate's inscription and the Jews' objection to it?

3. Describe the soldiers' actions regarding Jesus' garments.

4. What were Jesus' parting instructions to his mother and the disciple whom he loved?

5. Describe the moment of Jesus' death according to John.

## Dimension 2:
## What Does the Bible Mean?

### Pilate Considers Jesus' Innocence

John spins forth the dramatic telling of the denials of Peter, just as Jesus foretold. After Peter's third denial, John told how Jesus was taken to the praetorium, the official residence of a senior Roman magistrate of senatorial rank. The Jewish leaders did not follow into the pagan place, considered unclean for a Jew.

Religious authorities insisted that Pilate pronounce the death penalty since they had no authority to do so. Pilate asked Jesus if he were king of the Jews. The Jewish authorities had told Pilate that Jesus claimed to be the Messiah and the Messiah was usually thought to be the king of a people. Jesus asked Pilate if he thought the charges against him were justified. Pilate refused to commit himself. He could find no crime in Jesus, but he needed to placate the Jewish leaders. He could not get them to release Jesus, although it was the custom to release a condemned criminal at Passover (18:39).

Pilate had Jesus beaten, hoping the tortuous treatment would satisfy his accusers (19:1). The soldiers wove a crown of thorns and put a purple robe on Jesus, making fun of the claim to be king (19:2-3). Pilate spoke to Jesus

privately, attempting to find out more about why the Jews were so infuri-
ated with him (19:9). Jesus told Pilate that his power over him had been
ordained from God (19:11). Pilate dared not tolerate a rebel that some
claimed to be king.

At noon on the day of preparation for the Passover, Pilate handed Jesus
over to be crucified. To whom did Pilate hand Jesus? John implied that it was
to the Jewish chief priests. Later on he told us that it was Roman soldiers who
actually carried out the Crucifixion (19:23). A "pass the buck" atmosphere
existed. John seemed to indict both parties, the Jews and the Romans.

## The Crucifixion of Jesus

According to John, Jesus was processed outside the
city and forced to carry his own cross as was the
custom for the condemned.

He was led to "The Place of the Skull,"
Golgotha. No one knows for sure the origin of the
name. Three possible explanations are usually
given: it was the place of regular executions, it was
thought to be the burial place of Adam, or the hill
was shaped like a skull. The Latin form of
Golgotha is *Calvaria*. The word *Calvary* has

Pilate sat on the
judge's bench at "The
Stone Pavement,"
known also in Hebrew
as "Gabbatha." Today
this area, part of the
citadel adjacent to
Jaffa Gate, is consid-
ered the likely site of
Jesus' trial.

become synonymous with the cross. The site of the Crucifixion is near
Jerusalem. Tradition holds that the Church of the Holy Sepulchre was built
on the site.

## The Woman Stood With a Beloved Disciple

Most of the crowds and followers of Jesus were absent from the
Crucifixion, perhaps fearing for their own safety. John named some
women, including Jesus' mother and the disciple whom Jesus loved, as
standing near the cross. Depending on how one interprets the punctuation,
this could be two, three, or four women. It could mean that his mother was
Mary, wife of Clopas, and her sister was Mary Magdalene. It is unlikely
that two sisters were both named Mary. The verse could be read that three
women were present—Jesus' mother's sister was Mary of Clopas. Or it
could be understood as four women, two unnamed and two named. It is
not clear if Jesus' mother's sister is Salome of Mark 15:40 and Matthew
27:56. It was said Salome was the mother of James and John, the sons of
Zebedee, which would make them Jesus' cousins. The title, Mary
Magdalene, indicates Mary of Magdala, a town on the western shore of the
Sea of Galilee. She may be the sinful woman of Luke 7:37.

It has been suggested that the disciple whom Jesus loved may have been
the "other disciple" of 18:15-16 who went with Peter to the high priest.
This disciple was known in high places and therefore free to go where the

# CRUCIFIXION

The Roman practice of crucifixion may have been derived from the Persians. It was reserved for slaves or foreigners. To the Persians the earth was sacred. They believed that no dead thing should touch the earth, hence the practice of lifting the body above the earth until such time as the vultures and insects destroyed the flesh.

Originally the cross was an upright stake to which an already dead criminal was tied for display purposes. In time, a living body of a convicted criminal was attached to the cross, to await death. The Romans added a crossbar to the top of the stake for use during Roman crucifixions.

While there were variations from crucifixion to crucifixion, depending in part on the tastes of the executioner, the Romans standardized the practice to include several components.

- It was customary to flog or beat a victim, stripping the victim of clothing before the victim was lashed to a cross.
- When someone was nailed or lashed to a cross, no organs were damaged so it usually took several days of thirst, hunger, and pain before death occurred.
- A small wooden block supported the body, beneath the buttocks. The feet and hands were either tied or nailed to the cross.
- Crucifixion was intended to serve as a deterrent to further crime. Therefore, it occurred in a public place. In the crucifixion of Jesus, the event took place outside Jerusalem.
- It was customary to place a sign on the cross, indicating the offense of the criminal. The sign above Jesus' head read (in Latin, Greek, and Aramaic) "Jesus of Nazareth, the King of the Jews." The title is often depicted in art as I.N.R.I. which is an abbreviation of the Latin, *Iesus Nazarenus Rex Iudaeorum.* The Jews had placed Pilate in an awkward position. Perhaps he retaliated in his inscription declaring Jesus King. The chief priests objected to Pilate's sign, which appeared to mean that the Jews had approved of Jesus' kingship. They asked Pilate to change the sign. His famous reply was, "What I have written I have written" (19:22). Like Caiaphas' unconscious prophecy, Pilate had unwittingly given an honor to Jesus that would later be recognized as his universal sovereignty.
- The soldiers who executed a criminal were permitted to take his garments as part of

their pay. Four soldiers, according to John, divided Jesus' garments among themselves. He may have had four or five separate articles of clothing. They drew lots for his seamless tunic, fulfilling the words of Psalm 22:18.

- Jewish practice allowed for a crucifixion victim to be offered a drug to dull the pain. Jesus refused to dull the pain (Mark 15:23).

(Adapted from *Harper's Bible Dictionary*, edited by Paul J. Achtemeier, HarperCollins, 1985; page 194.)

others were not. This may account for his freedom to stand at the cross, when no other disciple was present. Jesus spoke to his mother, "Woman, here is your son" (26). He wanted her to regard the disciple as her own son and for the disciple to treat her as his own mother. The evangelist told us that from this point on, the disciple took Mary into his own family. In the spirit of protection and intercession that we have previously witnessed in Jesus, he asked the disciple to care for his mother.

## "I Am Thirsty"

Jesus indicated that he was thirsty (28). The writer saw this as another fulfillment of Scripture (Psalm 22:15; 69:21), possibly to indicate Jesus' full involvement in human life. A container of vinegar or sour wine, a popular drink of soldiers, was nearby. "They" (probably the soldiers) dipped a sponge in the liquid and put the sponge on the end of hyssop (a plant) to reach up to Jesus (29).

Some scholars point out that John intended the reference to hyssop because hyssop was used to sprinkle the blood of the paschal lamb on the doorposts of Israelite homes so that they would be passed over and spared (Exodus 12:22). John referred to hyssop, these scholars maintain, because of its symbolic quality. John portrayed Jesus as having died precisely at the time as the paschal lambs were sacrificed for the Passover meal. It is not clear if giving Jesus the sour wine was an act of mockery or of kindness.

The final words of Jesus, "It is finished" (30), declared that his earthly existence and work were done. These

words have the sense of consummation, completeness, and accomplishment rather than resignation. He bowed his head and "gave up his spirit" stressing the voluntary nature of his death.

## Particular Emphases of John

John had some particular concerns that may be addressed in terms of his variance from the accounts of the Crucifixion in the other Gospels. First, as mentioned earlier, Jesus carried his own cross, emphasizing his willing acceptance of his death. Second, while all the Gospels have a similar inscription over the cross, only John recorded that Pilate put it there or ordered it. Did John wish to convey the kingship of Jesus? Those who sought to kill Jesus ironically enthroned him. John also mentioned the seamless tunic not present in the Synoptics. It has been said that this tunic recalled priestly garb and so demonstrated Jesus' role as priest. This and some other details in John, such as the thirst, the sour wine, and the legs not being broken (19:33), were important because to John they fulfilled Scripture.

There are other differences from the Synoptics, such as the omission of the darkness over the land, the earthquake, the tearing of the Temple curtain, and no mention of the two persons crucified with Jesus. John added the inclusion of Jesus' words to his mother and the beloved disciple. These details reveal John's unique, succinct, and purposeful style in his telling of the enormity of Christ's death.

## Dimension 3:
## What Does the Bible Mean to Us?

### The Sovereignty of Christ

There are two prominent themes in John's story of the Crucifixion that are paramount to our understanding. One of those themes is the sovereignty of Christ. What does that say to us? Modern experience does not have the same understanding of kingship as during Jesus' time. Kings serve more as envoys, ambassadors, or even as figureheads today. Royalty is more of a curiosity to us than anything else. What was the kingship of Jesus, and why was it important? A public crucifixion was hideous. It was slow torture. The great paradox of the Christian faith is that instead of being unable to find God in such a hideous tragedy, it is precisely here that we are able to see God's glory more clearly than anywhere else. Here we see God's universal reign over humankind. It is not a kingship of oppressive rule. It is a sovereignty over everything—meaning and ultimacy above all. The religious leaders professed the supreme authority of another king—the worldly king, "Caesar." It is ironic that on

Passover, the commemoration of liberation from slavery to the Egyptian pharoah, a different ruler was deified, entrapping them in another form of slavery.

## The Protection and Care of Christ

Jesus' kingship is the kind that is related to care and protection. This is the second theme present in the Gospel of John. Like a good shepherd, Christ offers care. Like a priest, he intercedes for us. When Jesus turned over the care of his mother to the beloved disciple, it is usually assumed that the benefit was all Mary's—to be cared for and financially provided for. However, the deal was a "two-way street." Jesus said, "Woman, here is your son." She would provide for her new son what all mothers provide: nourishment, wisdom, spiritual guidance, and love. The new relationship that Jesus brought forth is one of this kind of care. Do we embody that new relationship in our treatment of one another?

Readers of this text may identify with Jesus, standing firm against opposition. As discussed in the last session, there are many examples of hostility against the message of Christianity. Yet we must not overlook the fact that there is probably something of the chief priests and even of Pilate within ourselves. We follow the crowd. We refuse to stand up for what is right. We may even demand or condone violence. We want to "pass the buck" and hand over the "dirty work" to others. We may reject the idea that we are like Pilate. He is usually pictured as evil, hypocritical, and pathetic. Yet who has never been in a "no-win" situation? We see in Pilate's decision-making process the tremendous pressure, the intense burden, of choice. While Pilate was fulfilling a role in John and carrying out a mission unbeknownst to him, we still get the sense of the desire not to have to decide at all. He could not say no to the Jewish leaders and still stay on their good side and maintain the status quo. Which of us has not succumbed to pressure at some time?

## Were You There?

There is a beautiful African American spiritual, "Were You There," the text of which asks the question, *Were you there when they crucified my Lord?* That hymn can remind us of the great sorrow of Jesus' death. It can also convict us. Although we may not have stood near the cross on that day so long ago, we still do to one another what was done to Jesus. The cross exposes our hatred, bigotry, and shortsightedness. "Sometimes it causes me to tremble, tremble, tremble. Were you there when they crucified my Lord?"

We are compelled to examine ourselves and our congregations. How can we weed out hate and plant seeds of love?

The religious leaders were meticulous about adhering to the laws of purification, yet they promoted the death of Christ not understanding what they were doing. We can be unmoving about things of little importance and yet so wishy-washy about things that matter most. We can get so involved in the proper conduct of matters that we lose sight of the way Christ calls us to live our lives. We can get so caught up in the "nuts and bolts" of things that we overlook the end we seek to accomplish. A popular slogan advocates, "The main thing is to keep the main thing, the main thing." Keeping things in perspective is one of the most challenging aspects of living.

Our efforts are aided as we keep the cross in the forefront of our lives. The cross is a revered symbol of Christianity, perhaps the most universally recognized symbol of our faith. The symbol has a history of its own and has taken many different forms. A simple cross—whether it be crudely carved in wood or made from a precious metal—evokes great meaning, tremendous feeling and a myriad of memories.

## Dimension 4:
## A Daily Bible Journey Plan

*Day 1:* **John 19:1-7**

*Day 2:* **John 19:8-12**

*Day 3:* **John 19:13-16a**

*Day 4:* **John 19:16b-30**

*Day 5:* **John 19:31-37**

*Day 6:* **John 19:38-42**

*Day 7:* **John 20:1-10**

# *I* HAVE SEEN THE LORD

## *What to Watch For*

As you read the Resurrection story in John 20, watch for the following events to be described:

➤ Jesus was taken down from the cross and laid in a tomb. Early on Sunday morning, Mary Magdalene went to the tomb. She found the stone had been removed and assumed someone had taken the body. Distraught, she told Simon Peter and the disciple whom Jesus loved of her suspicions. They too discovered the tomb to be empty. The beloved disciple followed Peter into the tomb and at that moment, we are told, he "believed "(8).

➤ The disciples returned home. Mary was left alone at the tomb. Looking inside, she saw two angels. Turning around, she found Jesus standing there. However, until he called her name, she did not recognize Jesus (16).

➤ Jesus said to her, "Do not hold on to me" (17). He told her to go tell the "brothers" (17) that his Ascension was near. Mary obeyed the call of Jesus, announcing "I have seen the Lord" (18), telling all that she had seen and heard.

This, according to John, was the first appearance of the risen Lord. Jesus would appear again to his disciples. John wrote to share the experiences of the witnesses so that those who would read his Gospel might come to believe.

1. What did Mary Magdalene see and think when she went to the tomb?

2. Upon hearing of the stone being removed, what did Peter and the beloved disciple do and see?

3. When the disciples left, what happened to Mary?

4. What were Jesus' instructions to her?

### The Burial of Jesus

Joseph of Arimathea asked permission from Pilate to take care of Jesus' body. According to Mark and Luke, Joseph was a member of the council that condemned Jesus. Luke told us that he disagreed with what the council had done. Matthew wrote that he was a disciple of Jesus. He and Nicodemus took Jesus' body, wrapped it in linen clothes, and laid it in a tomb. Matthew wrote that Joseph owned the tomb himself.

In John 20:1, we learn that Mary Magdalene went to the tomb early (it was still dark) on the first day of the week. Jesus had died on Friday. Saturday was the sabbath, and the law forbade going to a tomb on the sabbath. In the Synoptics several women went to the tomb. Mary Magdalene was included in all. John said she went alone, but in verse 2 she used the term *we*. Different explanations have been given for this. One is that the writer was combining several accounts that became confused. Another is that "we" in Greek sometimes was used instead of "I." The purpose for the women going to the tomb in the Synoptics was to complete the preparation of the body for burial. In John, Mary Magdalene was the only woman, and we are not told that she went to anoint the body. Presumably, she went because she was still grieving for Jesus.

The custom of mourning at a tomb was mentioned in John 11:31. It was customary to visit the tomb of a relative or loved one for three days after death. People believed that the spirit of the dead person hovered around the body for three days before leaving the body. In the other Gospels it was already light when the women went to the tomb. John may have it "still dark" to continue his contrast of light and dark, illustrating the darkness of Mary's grief. She saw the empty tomb, but did not yet see the "light" of the Resurrection.

Arimathea is a village in the hill country outside of Jerusalem. Home of Joseph, a follower of Jesus, the precise location of Arimathea is unknown. It has been identified with several modern cities, among them Rentis (east of Jaffa), er-Ram (north of Jerusalem), or el-Birah-Ramallah (north of Jerusalem).

*(From the Harper's Bible Dictionary; page 63.)*

# JESUS' TOMB

Although many other cultures of this period, among them the Romans, burned the bodies of the dead following a funeral, the Jews buried their dead. Wealthy Jews enlarged already existing caves to serve as tombs, sometimes lining them with limestone shelves to hold several bodies. Some of these tombs had a stone wheel that fit into a track across the entrance and served to close the doorway of the tomb. Such may have been the case in the tomb in which Jesus was interred, since the Gospel writers speak of a stone that needed to be rolled away before any could enter the tomb (Matthew 28:2; Mark 16:3; Luke 24:2; John 20:1).

As much as Christians might wish otherwise, the exact location of Jesus' tomb is not known. Tourists to Jerusalem learn that one conjectured location of the tomb is the Church of the Holy Sepulchre in Jerusalem.

*(Adapted from* Harper's Bible Dictionary; *page 1081.)*

## The Disciples Believed

Mary saw that the stone that normally blocked entrances to tombs in Palestine had been removed. She immediately assumed someone had taken the body. Grave robbery was common for several reasons. Someone may have wanted to inflict yet more humiliation on Jesus. Others may have believed that important personal effects of Jesus had been buried with him. Curiosity about the dead rabbi might offer yet a third reason. Regardless, Mary ran to tell Simon Peter and the disciple whom Jesus loved that the grave was open.

Peter went into the tomb followed by the other disciple. They found Jesus missing, but the linen clothes and the head cloth had been laid neatly aside. Upon this sight, the text says the beloved disciple believed. In what did he believe? Was it that Mary was telling the truth about the absence of the body?

That fact seems rather insignificant for the writer to point out so intentionally. It implied that this disciple believed that Jesus was risen, although, in the next verse it stated that they did not understand the Scripture when it said that he must rise. It may have occurred to him that if robbers had stolen the body they probably would not have left behind the linen. Some suggest that the way the burial clothes were lying may have indicated to the beloved disciple that the body was not stolen. (They were obviously not ripped off and tossed aside.) The description of the burial clothes might have been included to say that Jesus was leaving behind the clothes of the dead to emphasize life by contrast. The beloved disciple may not yet have fully grasped the meaning of the Resurrection according to verse 9, but at the sight of the discarded clothes in the empty tomb, he believed. The Gospel tells us that he already loved Jesus and was loved by him and believed in him. Now he believed in a new way, in a different way.

## Mary Magdalene Believed

The two disciples returned home. Mary Magdalene, who had gone back to the tomb, stood outside weeping. She grieved the death of her Savior. Her sadness was deepened by the loss of his body. She gazed into the tomb and saw two angels sitting at the head and foot of where Jesus had lain. They addressed her, "Woman, why are you weeping?" (13)

Mary turned around. Jesus appeared to her; she did not recognize him, exemplifying the pattern of misunderstanding in John. She thought he was the caretaker. This man also asked her why she was crying and who she was looking for. Possibly, Mary did not recognize him because of her tears or because she was preoccupied with the missing body. Mary asked if he was the one who had taken the body and volunteered herself to go and get it and bring it back. Jesus called her name, and it was at that moment that she recognized him.

It was common in most of the narratives of the appearance of the risen Jesus for there to be some difficulty in recognition. The Emmaus story in Luke 24:31-35 has the disciples walking with Jesus down the road before they recognized him. In John 21 the disciples did not recognize Jesus at once. The difficulty in recognition may have been to emphasize the notion that the witnesses were not expecting to see Jesus. They did not know that he was going to be resurrected. Also, the risen Jesus was quite different from the earthly Jesus and hence not immediately recognizable. We are told in Mark that the risen Jesus was in a different form. First Corinthians 15:42 discusses the nature of the difference in the resurrected body.

In her rush of recognition Mary breathed *"Rabbouni,"* an Aramaic word for "Teacher," "Master," or "Great One." She may also have reached out to touch him for Jesus said, "Do not hold on to me" (17), or as it is sometimes translated, "Do not cling to me, because I have not yet ascended to the Father" (17). What does this mean? It appears that Jesus prevented Mary from holding him, yet later invited Thomas to do so. This statement has been interpreted a number of ways. John may have meant to say that the physical touching of Jesus was not important. It is believing that counts. Touching for Mary was not necessary as it was for Thomas. Others have argued that there is a mistranslation here and what was really intended was something to the effect that Mary should not delay or linger, but go and tell the disciples before Jesus ascended to the Father. Still others think that since the phrase "do not hold me" is similar to the word for "do not be afraid" and since the other Gospels stress the fear of those who saw the risen Jesus, that this must have been a scribal error and "do not be afraid" was intended. In any case Jesus may not have been denying Mary something that he offered Thomas. We are to understand that Mary's relationship with Jesus had changed. His earthly ministry was over. He was telling her that she could no longer cling to the past. She was required to look upon him in a new way.

## Jesus Appeared to the Disciples

Jesus told Mary to go to "my brothers" and tell them what she had seen and to tell them about the Ascension. Jesus may have meant his blood relatives here, but it is likely he was referring to his disciples. There is not a separate Ascension event described here as in the Acts of the Apostles (1:3-11).

Ascension implies going up. It is spatial language that describes the completing of the exaltation and glorification, a process that had already begun.

Chapter 20 tells of an appearance of the risen Jesus to some disciples in a house in Jerusalem at the time that the Holy Spirit was given (20:22). Thomas was not with the disciples that evening, and when they told him that they had seen Jesus, he did not believe them. Jesus appeared to him also.

## The Purpose of This Book

We have what appears to be the end of the Gospel of John with the purpose of the book given. Most scholars believe that the original manuscript ended here in verse 31. Chapter 21 is an appendix, added at a later date and designed to describe another appearance to seven of the disciples by the Sea of Tiberius. Jesus shared a meal of fish and bread with them as he had done in John 6:1-13. The chapter concludes with Jesus' conversation with Peter and the beloved disciple concerning their mission. Peter had denied Jesus three times. Now he professed his love for Jesus three times. Jesus may have been foretelling a kind of martyrdom for Peter. Peter would bear witness even in the face of persecution. According to tradition, Peter was martyred in the persecution of Nero around A.D. 64. The writer saw the mission of the beloved disciple as that of a witness who would be around to testify to the truth of all these things.

## Dimension 3:
## What Does the Bible Mean to Us?

### A Jesus-Centered Faith
How does one even begin to approach a topic like the Resurrection? It is something so holy, so incomprehensible, so mysterious that even to try to explain it or teach it might suggest arrogance. Yet we are compelled to reflect on this central idea of the Christian faith; and when we look into John's telling of it, its power touches us anew.

Easter evokes a myriad of emotions and memories! Sorting out those emotions and memories against the backdrop of Scripture is an act of faith. The Resurrection has been called the climax of the Christ event, encompassing for Christians the meaning of life itself. It bears the burden of all human hopes, even giving us a reason for being.

The context for understanding the mystery of the Resurrection is in the ministry of Jesus. Jesus' preaching and teaching evoked strong emotions among the people that developed into a "Jesus-centered" faith. It is important to understand these strong emotions and responses of Jesus' followers in order to understand the Resurrection. The Resurrection did not force or coerce faith. It was more the realization that what Jesus was saying was true. It was a kind of breakthrough for the people of faith.

John made the people in this story, his witnesses, real and vivid. We see in them a spectrum of faith; they each have something to offer us.

### The Central Witness of Mary Magdalene
Why place Mary Magdalene in such a central role? Why was she given this crucial role in John? Why would she be the first witness? After all she was a woman, a Galilean. Why would this news be entrusted to her and her alone as John told it? In Mary Magdalene John showed that one of the "least," in terms of society's standards, could bring the news of such import. Sometimes

great things can come through the least expected, humblest means. Mary is an inspiration. Despite danger, fear, and sadness, she showed great courage.

How each of the individuals in the narrative came to believe in the Resurrection is important for us. The beloved disciple believed because of an empty tomb. Mary Magdalene believed because of Jesus' voice. Her spoken name evoked recognition. The disciples believed when they saw Jesus. And Thomas believed only when he was able to make physical contact with Jesus. These observations demonstrate that faith is different for everyone. Where are we in the spectrum?

> Faith does not stem from evidence or proofs; it is simply a gift from God. In John's Gospel to *believe* is not to accept a doctrine or a premise as true, but to be open and accepting, to have faith and trust in Jesus.

Mary was convinced that the body had been moved. Sometimes our fixed notions prevent us from seeing the truth. Do we tend to cling to our image of the earthly Jesus like a loved one who has died? Or do we accept the spiritual presence of Christ in our lives?

## Seeing Is Not Always Believing

Imagine Mary's despair turning to immense joy when she recognized Jesus. We see here the depths and heights of human feeling. She recognized Jesus when he called her by name. She saw Jesus but did not believe until she heard him. We each may believe that Jesus calls us personally. Jesus calls us and speaks to us in different ways. This story demonstrates that seeing is not always believing. It was not seeing that convinced Mary. John's message to his audience that was distanced from the event in time was that seeing is not necessary. John maintained that the possibility for faith is not limited to the small circle of witnesses to the risen Christ. Verse 29 is a blessing to all those who have not seen and yet who believe. We, too, join the crowd of witnesses who have not seen and yet believe.

Mary saw the risen Lord, but it was not the seeing that convinced her. Christianity is about "seeing" the Lord, meeting the Lord. It is the recognition of a spiritual presence in our lives. It is not keeping him at a safe distance, but allowing Jesus in, keeping Jesus close.

## What Does It Mean to Believe in the Resurrection?

What does it mean for us to believe in the Resurrection and accept the risen Savior? No one saw the actual Resurrection, but the Bible told of an empty tomb and some appearances of the risen Jesus. The earliest written evidence for the Resurrection is found in 1 Corinthians 15:3-8. Scholars believe these verses are a formula, almost like a creed, liturgy, or a catechism, a tradition that Paul is quoting. Paul probably received this tradition on a visit to Jerusalem around A.D. 38-40. The letter to the Corinthians is thought to have been written around A.D. 56-57. In this passage Paul said that "he was raised." It is in the passive voice, which seems to say that God acted. The words *to raise* in the Greek have a spatial dimension. The verse is used to describe one put on their feet again after a fall or one rising as from sleep. When used in the context of "to raise from the dead," the verb indicates a transition from one kind of existence to another. Chapter 15 of Corinthians probes the nature of the resurrected body of Jesus. The resurrected body will not be the same physical body. Resurrection is not the same thing as resuscitation. It is a much more radical transformation. The physical body is perishable. What is raised is imperishable.

The Resurrection means that death is no longer the last word. No more does death end life for us. Charles Wesley's hymn text expresses it well:

> Lives again our glorious King, Alleluia!
> Where, O death, is now thy sting? Alleluia!
> Once he died our souls to save, Alleluia!
> Where's thy victory, boasting grave? Alleluia!

To say that we are a Resurrection people or an Easter people is to say that together we are convinced of the reality and power of a risen Christ. Our lives are governed by that conviction. Resurrection faith is the knowledge that the Jesus of history sent from God is also the resurrected and exalted Christ in whom we believe and enter into a new relationship.

People of faith do not cling to the old ways of looking at things. People of faith see something beyond a mad rush to get as much as you can as fast as you can. Our hope is grounded in the Resurrection. The last word is not death, but life!

## Dimension 4:
## A Daily Bible Journey Plan

*Day 1:*  John 20:11-18
*Day 2:*  John 20:19-23
*Day 3:*  John 20:24-31
*Day 4:*  John 21:1-3
*Day 5:*  John 21:4-14
*Day 6:*  John 21:15-19
*Day 7:*  John 21:20-25

# GLOSSARY

*Ascension*—[uh-SEN-shuhn]
The return of Christ to heaven forty days after the Resurrection (Acts 1:6-11).

*Bethany*—[beth'uh-nee] A village on the east slope of the Mount of Olives, two miles east of Jerusalem. Jesus lodged here during the Passover week.

*Caiaphas*—[KAY-uh-fuhs] High priest at the time of Jesus. He instigated Jesus' arrest and trial before Pilate. Later he took part in the trial of Peter and John (Acts 4:1-22).

*Capernaum*—[kuh-puhr'nay-uhm] A city on the northern shore of the Sea of Galilee. Jesus made his home there after he moved from his ancestral village, Nazareth.

*Circumcision*—[SIR-kum-siz-shun] The process by which the prepuce of a male is removed. Circumcision is religiously observed by the Jewish faith, which understands it to be an outward sign of the covenant with God.

*Cross*—[kraus] An instrument of torture and execution, its use probably originated among the Persians and was adapted by the Romans as a punishment for slaves, for non-citizens, and occasionally for citizens guilty of treason.

*Cup*—Symbolizing the pleasant or bitter experiences of life, Jesus used it symbolically to refer to his Passion.

*Demon*—[DEE-muhn] A spirit with minor powers. The New Testament depicts demons as evil spirits exercising malevolent influences.

*Galilee*—[GAL-uh-lee] The northernmost region of ancient Israel, it was a region of Jews and Gentiles. Most of Jesus' ministry took place in Galilee.

*Gentiles*—[JEN-tighlz] A non-Hebrew (non-Israelite) person.

*Gethsemane*—[geth-SEM-uh-nee] The place where Jesus went to pray during the night on which he was betrayed.

*Gospel*—[GOS-puhl] (1) Good news concerning Christ, the kingdom of God, and salvation. (2) One of four books—Matthew, Mark, Luke, and John—containing the authorized story of the life and teachings of Jesus.

*Jerusalem*—[ji-ROO-suh-luhm] The city of David, holy city of Judaism, Christianity, and Islam. Many of the events of Jesus' last days took place in or near Jerusalem.

**Jordan**—[JOR-duhn] The largest and most important river in Palestine, extending over two hundred miles from its sources near Mt. Hermon in the north to its outlet in the Dead Sea. During part of his public ministry Jesus traveled along the eastern bank of the river, and he crossed it at Jericho as he began his final journey to Jerusalem.

**Judea**—[joo-DEE-uh] The Greek and Latin form of Judah. During New Testament times Judea was used loosely to refer to nearly all of Palestine.

**Manna**—[MAN-uh] Food on which the Israelites subsisted during the wilderness wanderings. A day's supply appeared each morning (Exodus 16). An important symbol of God's faithful response to human beings. The gift of manna and the multiplying of bread and fish were seen in nearly the same light. Both were gifts of a saving God.

**Messiah**—[muh-SIGH-uh] Literally "anointed one": "Messiah" from the Hebrew, "Christ" from the Greek. Messiah refers specifically to Jesus' vocation to "save his people from their sins." His anointment was actually his calling by God to his ministry of preaching, teaching, and healing.

**Moses**—[MOH-zis] The Hebrew leader who led the Exodus from Egypt. Moses received the Ten Commandments at Mount Sinai; led the Hebrews through the wilderness for forty years; and died on Mount Nebo after viewing the Promised Land. Because of his prominence and his role in the act of salvation, Jesus is sometimes referred to as the "Second Moses."

**Nazareth**—[NAZ-uh-rith] A city in Galilee where Jesus grew up. Mary and Joseph settled here when they returned from Egypt. Jesus moved from Nazareth to Capernaum at the beginning of his public ministry. He returned at least once to his boyhood home, where his message was rejected.

**Nicodemus**—[nik-uh-DEE-muhs] Pharisee and member of the Sanhedrin who went to Jesus by night to ask questions (John 3:1-21). He asked the Sanhedrin if the law could condemn a man unheard (John 7:32-52). He helped Joseph of Arimathea bury Jesus (John 19:38-42).

**Pharisees**—[FAIR-uh-seez] A movement within Judaism of the late Second Temple period (150 B.C.-A.D. 70). The Pharisees were noted most for their strict observance of the Jewish religion, their accurate exposition of the law, their handing down of extra-biblical customs and traditions, their moderate position with regard to the interplay of fate and free will, and their belief in the coming resurrection and in angels.

**Priest**—A mediator between God and humankind, who instructed the people in God's laws concerning conduct and worship. The priest officiated in the offering of sacrifices. After the destruction of the Davidic monarchy, the priestly hierarchy in Jerusalem took over the political as well as the religious leadership of the people. Neither Jesus nor his disciples rejected the legitimacy of the priesthood and sacrifices.

**Sabbath**—[SAB-uhth] The seventh day of the week, observed as a day of rest in Israelite and Jewish religion since earliest times. The controversies in which Jesus was involved with regard to the sabbath all hinged on his authority as a teacher over against the Pharisees' interpretations of sabbath laws or on the legality of redemptive acts normally forbidden as work on the sabbath.

**Sadducees**—[SAD-joo-seez] A sect existing within Judaism from some time in the second century B.C. to A.D. 70. They were the party of those with political power. They accepted only the written Torah and rejected all oral interpretation of tradition. They rejected the doctrine of the future resurrection, belief in angels and spirits, and views of the Pharisees. Their influence among the common people was quite limited.

**Samaritans**—[suh-MAIR-uh-tuhnz] The inhabitants of the region of Samaria and adherents of the Samaritan religious tradition. Samaritans came to be regarded as neither fully Gentile nor fully Jewish. "Samaritan" could itself be a term of contempt among Jews.

The Samaritan's Scripture contained only the Pentateuch. They regarded Moses as the final prophet of God and a superhuman being. Samaritans appear in positive roles in Jesus' teaching and the record of his ministry.

**Sanhedrin**—[san-HEE-druhn] A council in Jerusalem that functioned as the central judicial authority for Jews. Ideally the Sanhedrin included seventy members plus the high priest who served as the president. It was composed of representatives of the leading priestly families and the religious instructors known as "scribes." Also included were "elders" who were not connected with the scribes or priests.

**Scribes**—[skribz] Interpreters and teachers of the Mosaic law. The scribes came to be addressed with respectful titles, particularly "Rabbi" (meaning "my master," "my teacher"). At the root of the conflict between Jesus and the scribes lay the question of his independent interpretation of the Scriptures (Torah).

**Sea of Galilee**—The larger of the two lakes in northern Palestine, located in the region in which Jesus conducted most of his public ministry. The lake is thirteen miles long and eight miles wide at its widest point. It is where Jesus called his first disciples. He crossed and recrossed it frequently during his ministry.

111

**Shepherd**—[SHEP-hurd] A common occupation in ancient Palestine, often used metaphorically in biblical narratives. Because shepherds were the sole source of provisions and protection for sheep in the ancient Near East, *shepherd* came to be applied to God, who guides and cares for the people. Jesus was called a Shepherd as the leader and guardian of his people, as the one who suffered for his people, and as the final judge of the nations.

**Sin**—The failure of human beings to live the life intended for them by God, their creator. Sin in its basic sense is always ultimately against God rather than against humankind. The fundamental effect of sin is alienation between God and the person or society that sins. Reconciliation is the heart of what is accomplished in God's salvation of humankind. God initiates the process of reconciliation, but a human response to God's action is always required.

**Son of Man**—A favorite expression of Jesus in the Gospels. It is used by Jesus to describe his ministry and authority on earth, to predict his suffering and death, and to refer to his coming as the judge of the nations at the end of the age.

**Synagogue**—[SIN-uh-gog] Buildings used for Jewish worship and instruction in the Scriptures. They came into being during the Persian period (539-330 B.C.). In time the synagogues came to be the focal point of Judaism. After the destruction of the Temple in A.D. 70, the synagogue made possible the survival of Judaism. The synagogues were the center of the Jewish community in any town with a Jewish population and were used for political functions, including judgment of Jewish violators of the Jewish law.

**Synoptic Gospels**—[sin-OP-tik GOS-puhlz] The first three Gospels of the New Testament, which coordinate closely. They do not include the Gospel of John.

**Temple**—[TEM-puhl] Solomon built the first Temple in Jerusalem between 958 and 954 B.C. The Babylonians burned it to the ground in 587/586 B.C. Efforts to rebuild it began in 537 B.C. and it was restored in 520 B.C. In 20-19 B.C. Herod dismantled it and began to replace it with one of grander design constructed in Hellenistic-Roman style. It was destroyed by the Romans in A.D. 70 and never rebuilt.

**Twelve**—Another word used to describe the disciples of Jesus Christ. They are usually referred to as "the Twelve."

Adapted from *Bible Teacher Kit* © 1994 by Abingdon Press.

CPSIA information can be obtained at www.ICGtesting.com
Printed in the USA
LVOW06s0815110815

449577LV00001B/1/P